Automobilia

Leila Dunbar

Schiffer Publishing Ltd ®

4880 Lower Valley Road, Atglen, PA 19310 USA

Acknowledgments

To Howard and Martha: Thanks for taking me out on all those auto excursions, letting me sleep in the back seat! It's obvious that my love of cars was born early. To Noel Barrett Auctions and Bob and Judy Palmerino: Thank you for letting me use photos from your long-time labor of love collection. I'm sure it was not easy seeing it leave your home. To all of our consignors, customers, collectors, and dealers with whom we've dealt over the past twenty-five years, thank you for your support. Without it, we would not have these great examples to show off in this book. After all, the hunt is a lot of fun, but what's more intriguing are the adventures encountered and characters met during the journey.

Copyright © 1998 by Leila Dunbar
Library of Congress Catalog Card Number: 98-85220

Designed by Bonnie M. Hensley
Layout by Randy L. Hensley
Typeset in Americana XBd BT/Times New Roman

ISBN: 0-7643-0624-3
Printed in Hong Kong
1 2 3 4

Published by Schiffer Publishing Ltd.
4880 Lower Valley Road
Atglen, PA 19310
Phone: (610) 593-1777; Fax: (610) 593-2002
E-mail: Schifferbk@aol.com
Please write for a free catalog.
This book may be purchased from the publisher.
Please include $3.95 for shipping.

In Europe Schiffer books are distributed by
Bushwood Books
6 Marksbury Avenue
Kew Gardens
Surrey TW9 4JF England
Phone: 44 (0) 181 392-8585; Fax: 44 (0) 181 392-9876
E-mail: Bushwd@aol.com

Please try your bookstore first.

We are interested in hearing from authors
with book ideas on related subjects.

Contents

Introduction

The Kid and the Junkyard

When I was a little kid, I spent a lot of time fishing cars in my dad's junkyard. (I think this fully explains why I'm not a software programmer or hairdresser today.) In those days, the late '60s-early 1970s, cars would be towed in, chock full of stuff left behind in the wake of the ambulance or police car. The dismantling guys might pick up anything from shoes to tapes to undergarments.

On a good day, I could make five dollars in change just by searching the interiors. That would buy a lot of baseball cards in those days. In the summer, if the car had been sitting a while, wasps might build nest, or a snake would be disturbed, adding to the danger factor, and excitement. Occasionally a coin would have some dried blood or foreign matter on it (remember, these cars had been in accidents), nothing that a little soap couldn't wash away. If I wanted to really throw the store clerk, I'd just hand it to them and see what they would do.

This is where I started learning about cars. My dad always ran an American-make-only junkyard. In 1972, he chose to sell General Motors parts exclusively and our place became the boutique of junkyards. If no one else had it, we did. Our yard was always clean, the cars in neat rows. To dismantle the drivetrain, our Catepillar loader would lumber up the row like a hefty nurse, hoist the vehicle on its forks and carry it back to the shop, where it would be gently let down and worked on with an airwrench—no torches. It was organized, neat, ahead of its time. The guys could have been wearing white lab coats as they extracted parts to keep other cars on the road, for a price of course.

As a teen, I drove Trans Ams, Monte Carlos, Berlinettas, and Suburbans. My friends loved me—the last one to get a license, the first one to get a car. After school, I delivered used parts or cleaned repaired cars that were going on the lot. I had a 1970 GTO convertible, with a 4-speed, that had more plastic in it than an aging actress. We finally sold it after my dad drove it sideways up the street after a sudden rainstorm. We probably beat the accident odds with that car. My favorite car, however, was a 1970 Orange Cutlass (that you'll hear about later) with a 455 motor and an 8-track. We still have that car today, with only 68,000 miles, along with a 1972 Cutlass convertible, and don't plan on selling either one.

My dad started collecting old signs and toys when the business became a large pinball machine: four phones ringing, four teletypes spitting out part requests, five guys and a secretary waiting for orders, motors revving, air wrenches whirling—an automotive cacophony. He had to get out and relax. So he took the back seat out of a 1973 Mercury Marquis, put my mom in the passenger's seat and took off to find the past. Soon, a Pegasus pointed the way to parts. Next thing we all knew, Olds, Chevy, Cadillac, Pontiac, and Buick signs livened up our formerly dull grey buildings.

They were nice, but I really didn't care about antiques until my twenties. In high school and college I was too consumed with other hobbies—sports, music, and men. My turn was to come later. I finally decided I liked old signs when I felt a pang selling a rare 1920s Acheson Lubricants poster to a good friend of ours. I loved the scene with the woman by the car, in duster, hat, and scarf, waiting for the mechanic to finish his work so she could go on her way.

In college, majoring in journalism and Spanish, I drove a Camaro, then a prime 1977 Cutlass S, forest green with tan bucket interior, 260 with a 5-speed, a beautiful car. I returned from college not knowing what career I really wanted to pursue, but I knew I wanted a car with T-tops. So they built the Camaro for me, while I sold the Cutlass. Foolish girl. The jerk who bought the Cutlass trashed it, while I decided that T-tops weren't the be-all in life (although I really like sunroofs now). I guess this is how we grow up.

I thought I would stay at the yard for a year to pay back my parents for sending me to school. At this time my dad was doing all the buying and the selling. So, I learned how to buy car wrecks at auction. On a typical Monday, it would be fifty-five guys with blue or green uniforms on, and me, in jeans, usually with some kind of battery acid hole or grease mark showing through the denim. It's just not a clean business, no matter how hard you try to remain immaculate.

In six months, I became very good at buying. I knew our inventory, I knew what we needed, I knew what I could spend. I didn't have a lifetime of petty greivances built up with the other bidders, so they let me alone. If a car went for more than what I was willing to pay, I just let it go. Another one would come along.

I found, to my surprise, that I liked it. I drove in, I checked out the vehicles, I bought, I left and had lunch (in the old days, the boys would have a few belts at the local bar and restaurant, my father tells me, but that wasn't my thing), took a drive, saw my boyfriend, and got back to the yard in time to inventory the new wrecks being delivered.

Unfortunately, by the 1980's, the cars were pretty well fished out and stripped by the time they hit the yard. I was lucky if I could scrape a dime from under the front seat.

In a world always screaming about sexual harrassment and litigation, I never had a comment made or felt uncomfortable because I was a woman, though I was usually the only female at the auction. Of course, that could have to do with the fact that they all knew my dad. However, I like to think that they were gentlemen in this regard and will keep that thought with me.

Because of soap opera circumstances that will not be detailed here (wait for the Kitty Kelley book), involving an aborted romance (some men just don't appreciate a woman who knows the difference between a 305 and 350 Chevy motor), I stayed for five years instead of one, buying cars, inventorying the yard, selling parts, delivering parts, and taking off parts when needed.

Dad bought lots more signs, more toys, more stuff. We both tired of the junkyard business at the same time, he after 34 years, me after five. More complex cars, less interchange, higher insurance, dismantler turnover, competition with stolen parts and repair shop scams, ... combined to take the fun out of the business. It was time to move on.

So, like many collectors, we became full-time dealers. Eleven years later, after doing the show circuit and handling a mailorder business, we now run auctions in automotive and motorcycle memorabilia, with a worldwide clientele. And, you'll be pleased to know that we run our business out of our former junkyard. There's a Packard Sign on the front building, and a Speedway neon sign hanging from Building Number 2. Most of the car wrecks are long gone, just a few are kept for our licenses. We do have a very cool 1968 Delta 88 GM-Delco demo show car, with all the Delco attributes, such as shocks that keep the car on an even plane, etc., and of course, our Cutlasses.

That is our story. All collectors have these stories about why they were drawn into collecting, and I thought you should know ours. This book is for all collectors, whether you started your automotive love affair with a Moon, a Nash or a Chevy.

How to Start Collecting

There are some very important tenets to follow in collecting,whether it's signs or spoons, because you are going to see the same piece at some show three times in three different conditions and it's going to have three different prices. You need to know how to make good decisions in your buying.

If you are a beginner collector, note that there are risks inherent in collecting. Like driving the Indy 500, it's not for the faint of heart and shouldn't be jumped into by the inexperienced. Just because you have a flame retardent jumpsuit and a helmet doesn't make you a racecar driver (I think there's a country song about this).

To build a solid collection and to ensure a pleasant experience, you must take the time to learn about the collectibles market and what segment you want to collect. You need to meet and develop relationships with other collectors and dealers. How do you do this? Start with the Yellow Pages. Find out who deals in your area. Once you hit a shop, you'll see that the dealer usually knows about the shows and auctions going on. Also, almost always, there will be trade publications in his shop, with local shows and auctions listed. Start going to the shows and auctions. Be friendly, ask questions. Soak up the atmsosphere. Listen to how deals are made. Check out the prices. You'll start making friends and becoming part of the scene.

And, above all, make sure you buy things that you like. You are the person who's going to live with them. What's the point of a good deal when you don't like the piece? Once you know what you like, find out what books and publications carry the items you're looking for. Find out what's common and rare. Learn the price ranges of poor condition to mint condition.

Once you feel comfortable, then make your first buy, preferably from someone you've met, with whom you've developed a relationship. You'll find that your best buys in the long run come from doing business with the same people. They are more likely to give you a better price break than strangers. Remember, too, that a number of dealers do this for a living (like us). If you treat them with respect, they will treat you the same. If you constantly whine when negotiating a deal, they will be less likely to give you a break and/or put aside the best pieces for you. It's the old honey and bee syndrome.

Finally, buy the best condition that you can afford. The biggest mistake that beginning collectors make is that they buy pieces in poor condition because they're cheaper, instead of spending the extra money for the same items in excellent condition. They're afraid to spend too much. Just the opposite is true. The items bought in great condition are the ones that will hold their value over time. If you do your homework, it won't take you long to figure out when you should stretch and spend for that rare piece in great condition.

Until you become comfortable in your collecting skills, the good news is that there are many historic collectibles that are still affordable for beginners and/or those with Chevette pocketbooks. Later pins, from '30s through the present, can still be had for a few dollars. The very early celluloid pins with short-lived car makes are the expensive ones. Shoot for the later metal pins and build a nice collection. Lots of automotive paper, i.e., dealership literature and manuals, are also very reasonable, as are many magazines. There are still signs to be had for $50-$200. They just won't be the rarest of the rare.

Notes About Pricing and the Purpose of this Book

The purpose of this book is to give a good overview of a number of automotive collectibles, from toys to advertising to smalls. Most books concentrate on only dealership materials, or only gas and oil, or only toys, or only advertising. In this book, we try to incorporate them all as they were produced at the same time and the fortunes of one area coincided with the others.

Instead of writing long chapter introductions, I've chosen to put more details into each description. I think putting bite-size bits of information with each photo makes it easier to study and gives relevancy to each piece.

Pricing is the hardest part of this book and my least favorite, because no matter how much experience you have, how many places you've been, and how much you've read, it's impossible to know everything that's going on and to be completely accurate. Furthermore, like any market, stock or otherwise, collectibles go through cycles and fluctuations. Condition, rarity, and current desirability mean everything in valuation.

I set wide value ranges on purpose. Why? Because condition is the cornerstone of value. If a rare sign in mint condition brings $6,000, it doesn't mean one in a #5 condition will bring $5,000. More likely, it will be in the $1,000-1,500 range, because the most serious collectors, the ones with the most money, want the signs in the best condition. They know those will appreciate the most in the long run. If that same sign is in poor condition, it could be worth $500. That is what makes this collecting business so tricky. Also, note that I tried to set the range on the lower side—I'd rather be conservative than off the deep end.

Restoration is becoming more widely accepted, particularly for rare signs that otherwise would not survive. How does restoration affect the value of a sign? It depends on the quality of the restoration. There are not many accomplished restorers in this field, and it's not a widespread practice. Probably the best rule of thumb to follow is that a nicley restored sign is worth about half of what the sign would be in excellent original condition.

Finally, please remember that *there is no such thing as a set-in-stone price guide*. The prices in this book are simply to be used as a rough guideline. I and the publisher will not be responsible for differences between this book and and what happens in real life. Markets and collecting whims change too quickly. It is each collector's responsibility to be informed.

Reference books can be helpful in determining relative values, but that's it. The real determination of the current market is out there at the swap meets, antique shows, and auctions. So make sure you ask questions and finger the goodies. Books educate, but they don't buy and sell—people do.

When you go forth, remember what your investing your time, money and energy in—building a collection that reflects your personality and character, amassing items that you will have around you every day, and developing relationships with like minded people.

Chapter 1

Signs

Buick, Texaco, Ford, Goodyear, and Shell. These companies were born in the early 1900s as America shifted from oat-fed to oil-led horsepower. Nine decades after the first curved-dash Oldsmobile rolled out of its makeshift factory, automotive sign collectors today will pay far more for that Olds sign over the door than the first production motorcar's $850 price tag.

The hobby of collecting vintage automotive porcelain and tin signs has shifted into big business overdrive for the same reason Al Unser Jr. wears a Marlboro patch on his flame retardant jumpsuit--money.

Like most hobbies concerning collectibles, auto sign values have accelerated steadily during the past two decades. Fifteen years ago we bought a 1950s Texaco Marine White Porcelain Pump Sign at a show (in the afternoon!) for $20. The same sign is now worth $450-$850, depending on condition.

The sign market boomed in the mid- to late-1980s. Disposable income flowed like pre-Saudi gas into petroleum-related signs. Then, in 1990-91, the economy faltered and so did the automotive sign market, culminating in a Richard Oliver Transportation Auction where some of the strongest buyers became sellers. Without their support in bidding, many items stalled and were left helplessly by the side of the road.

For the past three years, automotive excitement has geared up again. Not only are hoards of collectors attending the traditional Hershey and Iowa gas bashes, but mini gas meets have popped up in Columbus, Ohio, New York, and now Massachusetts. Mainstream publications like *USA Today* have been prompted to write articles about the burgeoning sign collectible market .

What has caused this screeching U-turn? There are two very basic reasons—an improved auto-economy and the monkey-see, monkey-do factor. First, most automobilia collectors (the majority of whom are men) work in some aspect of the automotive industry, and the attraction extends beyond work hours. A sky's-the-limit stock market has sent car owners racing to their friendly automotive dealerships, to buy new models or to spruce up or restore their classic beauties. Better business means more bucks for collectors to spend on their motor mistresses.

What's healthy is that many new people are coming into the hobby and giving it a jumpstart. Bread and butter signs, such as Flying A and Mobil pump signs, are not rare but are very popular and whet the beginning collectors' appetite to move up to more unusual Gargoyle or Tidewater Associated signs and well beyond.

Secondly, collectors are gaining confidence in the market after spending time watching their friends stepping up and paying the price to buy the pick of the lot, be it through dealers, longtime collections, or auctions. This enthusiasm translates into a willingness to put the pedal to the metal and buy a more expensive sign that they might not have stretched for otherwise. Time has proven that the best signs appreciate the most rapidly and most dramatically, so that the extra money is usually well invested.

What's hot? Conservative collectors prefer the stability of the big blue chips of oil and gas—Shell, Texaco, Gulf, or Mobil. Others want the regional pioneering brands with great logos, some of which were just a tiny spurt in the gas geyser, like Oilzum, Signal, Gilmore, Richfield, and Red Crown.

Vintage and sports car owners want dealership signs that they can hang over their collectible cars, and the range is similiar, from the longtime familiar favorites of GM and Ford, to the extinct and more exotic Hudson, Packard, and Reo brands.

Tire signs that roll out such formidable names as Michelin and Goodyear and battery signs such as Eveready and Columbia are chased after by collectors, particularly those showing whitewalls spinning and cells igniting. Once ignored, charge and credit card signs, automotive insurance signs, and no smoking signs (certain Shell and Texaco No Smoking signs are in the $1,000-1,500 range) are now coveted as much as their gas and oil counterparts.

For all signs, like automobiles themselves, rarity, condition, and great graphics determine the value scale. A good rule of thumb is to buy the best condition that you can afford. The greatest demand will always be for the rarest and most dynamic signs in the best condition. Junk is almost always junk, until someone figures out a way to make it art.

Where will the sign market go? We have been collecting and dealing for twenty years and think that the market will maintain its pace and become even stronger because there are only so many good pieces to go around, with many signs already locked away in collections. As long as new collectors bring clout into the marketplace and current collectors maintain faith, the market will remain bullish.

What threatens the market? If the driving public decides to trade in their wheels for transit passes (not likely) or stops clamoring for repairs and new cars, the automotive business will hit a large speed bump and disposable income will shrink like a GTO's gas mileage, forcing the sign market to run on less fuel.

Also, if prices shoot up so high that Jed Clampett has a problem affording signs, the monkey see factor will again come into effect as collectors get scared and decide to cash out. Right now, the solid middle-of-the-road porcelain signs are currently selling for $300-1,500. If this price structure pushes too far too fast (and it has begun in the even rarer aviation and marine gas/oil signs, with scarce examples now selling for $3,000-6,000), buyers will become sellers.

The other threat to the market is the occasional appearance of dealers without scruples. If a collector has a bad experience because he unknowingly buys a reproduction, or if the sign he has purchased is not in the condition that he has been told, his confidence is undermined and he loses enthusiasm. This hurts all of us, dealers and collectors alike. Make sure you get a guarantee of authenticity and a right of return before buying from someone whom you don't know. The number of unethical dealers is very small and they are found out very quickly in this tiny hub of a hobby.

Overall, the market is humming like a Viper on a Nevada highway, with long open stretches in sight. New collectors are joining the circle, books about automotive signs are in the works, and great signs are being bought, sold, displayed, and appreciated.

With all this recent attention focused on the automotive collectible world and the recent rise of collectibles shows and magazines, don't be surprised if you're channel surfing one night and find sandwiched between the Talladega 500 and *Melrose Place* an Oprah special on Michelin—Men Who Are Addicted to Automobilia and the Women Who Love Them.

Dealership Signs

Blue Ribbon Durant—Dort Carriage Co., Flint, Michigan, Wooden Sand Sign, Circa 1905, Dark Blue & Silver, Framed, 8' x 1'. *Courtesy of Dunbar's Gallery.* $500-2,000, Extremely rare.

William Durant, founder of General Motors, was not an engineer, but an entrepreneur. While a traveling insurance salesman in the 1880s, Durant paid $50 for the patent for a new style of horse-drawn cart. By the late 1890s, he had made millions, selling more than 150,000 Durant-Dort carriages a year. This success and his forward thinking inspired him to enter into the next realm of technology, automobiles.

Durant wooden sand sign, circa 1921-23, framed, 36" x 31". *Courtesy of Dunbar's Gallery.* $300-700, Scarce.

William Durant first bought out David Buick's floundering company in 1905, and by 1908 was the leading seller in the fledgling industry. He incorporated General Motors in 1908, buying out other companies so fast that it created a huge cash flow deficit. He was pushed out of the presidency in 1910, only to take back that position when GM merged with Chevrolet, another company he started, in 1915. Durant enjoyed a few more years of success, until a post World War I recession hit in 1920, and he was ousted a second time. This time he chose, again, to start a new company, with his own name, just a few weeks after leaving GM. He made a number of cars, including the Star, Eagle and Flint, with four- and six-cylinder motors, in the $850 range. However, they didn't capture the public's imagination. Durant never repeated his earlier triumphs and went out of business in 1932.

GMC neon porcelain sign without the neon, circa 1935, 67" x 44" with 1" lip, by Texlite. *Courtesy of Dunbar's Gallery.* $500-1,500.

GMC Trucks, working two-color neon porcelain sign, deco effect via diecut process, 66" x 44" x 6-3/4", circa 1930, with Bolt One GMC circle, by Walker & Co. *Courtesy of Dunbar's Gallery.* $1,500-4,500.

Walker & Co. of Detroit was one of the major signmakers for General Motors in the 1920s-30s. With the evolution of neon in the 1920s, and the competition between companies to make their agencies stand out, it was inevitable that neon would be the sign of choice for the Deco era. GMC trucks were the workhorses of the GM line and the unsung heroes that helped the company get through tough times. Businesses always needed tough, reliable delivery and construction vehicles, and GMC obliged.

GMC Trucks neon counter sign, circa 1930, 18"diameter. Indoor counter sign with spinning light designed to get customer's attention. *Courtesy of Dunbar's Gallery.* $300-800.

GMC Trucks double-dided porcelain sign, circa 1926-28, 30" diameter. *Courtesy of Dunbar's Gallery.* $500-1,200.

GMC Trucks porcelain sign, double sided, circa 1928-30, 42" diameter. $500-1,000. *Courtesy of Dunbar's Gallery.*
  Note color difference between years, GMC signs are always sought after by collectors.

GMC parts porcelain sign, circa 1940s, Walker & Co., 30" x 36". *Courtesy of Dunbar's Gallery.* $300-900.

Buick Motor Cars-Valve In Head tin sign, circa 1925, wood frame, 47" x 47". *Courtesy of Dunbar's Gallery.* $500-1,000.
  David Buick, who emigrated from Scotland, was originally a bathtub manufacturer who developed a process for adhering porcelain to iron, a process that the British had held secret. Based in Detroit, he made a fortune in the late 1890's, and, like many entrepreneurs, looked for another challenge. He sold out and teamed up with designer Eugene Richard, who created the valve-in-head engine used to this day in Buicks. Valve-in-head engines have a valve over the piston, which creates more power, a faster burn, and more compressed combustion. Unfortunately, his research also burnt up all his capital. By 1904, Buick was up to the tops of his valves in debt, with no relief in sight, until William Durant came along, test drove Buick's car and bought him out. Buick moved to Los Angeles and started an oil company that failed, while Durant used Buick as the foundation of General Motors.

Buick Motor Cars porcelain thermometer, circa 1912-20, 7" x 28", *Courtesy of Dunbar's Gallery.* $200-700.
  The name Buick immediately conjures the image of quality, power and conservative good looks. (Sounds like a young banker, doesn't it?) Before Walter Chrysler left in 1920 to head his own company, he was the head of the Buick division.

Buick's the Buy, 1930s showroom poster with Santa, 30" x 40".
Courtesy of Dunbar's Gallery. $100-350.

Buicks were restyled in 1929, including the addition of hydraulic shocks and increased engine power. In 1931, straight 8 motors were used in all models with a corresponding price increase, a decision made before the stock market crash which cost Buick a good chunk of its customer base for the first years of the Depression.

Better Buy Buick 1930s trolley card, 20" x 12". *Courtesy of Dunbar's Gallery.* $75-200.

By the late 1930s, Buick had reclaimed much of its clientele, moving up to fourth in production by 1938. Buick introduced the first flashing electric turn signals in 1939, installed on the back of the car as part of the trunk emblem.

Buick Valve in Head porcelain sign, single sided, 20" diameter. *Courtesy of Dunbar's Gallery.* $200-600.

In GM's marketing strategy of being all things to all customers, Buick was the model aspired to by those who first purchased a Chevy, then Pontiac, then Olds. Buick customers were professionals who didn't need the ultimate status of a Cadillac.

Buick Authorized Service porcelain sign, double sided, circa 1940s, 42" diameter. *Courtesy of Dunbar's Gallery.* $300-90.

During the 1940s (before and after World War II), Buick was GM's number two maker after Chevrolet, producing 300,000 cars a year. World War II again was bad timing for Buick, interrupting its momentum, as GM super designer Harley Earl had just finished a stunning makeover for Buick, sleek, wide, and low, the words GM would be following for the 1950s.

Buick Quick Service double-sided porcelain sign, circa 1940s, 26" x 16". *Courtesy of Dunbar's Gallery.* $200-600.

For GM, styling always seemed to come before actual service, a concept that would haunt them come the 1980s' influx of quality Japanese imports.

Cadillac Service porcelain sign, with shield logo, 60" diameter. *Courtesy of Dunbar's Gallery.* Excellent condition, $600-1,800.

Known as the top of the line in the GM auto hierarchy, Cadillac was part of the original incorporation of GM in 1909 by William Durant. Henry Leland, at 60 years old and a superior engineer, took over the Detroit Automobile company in 1904, after leaving Oldsmobile. He developed a new car and named it after a French explorer who built a fort in what later became Detroit. The quality of Cadillac was based on Leland's fanaticism with the pursuit of excellence, which gave birth to the motto

"The Standard of the World." Durant bought Cadillac in 1909, another thoroughbred for his iron stable. For the past ninety years, Cadillac has remained a symbol of wealth and status, a car to strive to own. Cadillac defined the space age look of many 1950s vehicles, the first to sport tail fins in 1948. Harley Earl was inspired by the Lockheed P-38 fighter plane and soon every automaker was turning their models into road jets. Many amenities and developments that were considered luxurious, such as air suspension in 1957, were first tried on the Cadillac.

Cadillac/LaSalle porcelain sign, double sided, with shield logos, Walker & Co., Detroit, circa 1930s, 30" x 24" *Bob & Judy Palmerino Collection; Courtesy of Noel Barrett Auctions.* Very rare, particularly with combination of both LaSalle and Cadillac, $1,000-4,000.

You could think of the LaSalle as the forerunner to Cadillac's "cheap" line of Cimarrons in the early 1980s. Harley Earl, head of design, conceived of the car as a less expensive alternative the Cadillac. Sold for $2,495 in 1927, it was hardly competition for the Model A. As the '30s wore on, it was continually cheapened, both in quality and price, but was still squeezed out by 1940, as the more basic Cadillac models were only slightly more expensive.

Chevrolet Genuine Parts bow-tie diecut porcelain sign, circa 1930s, 24" x 20". *Courtesy of Dunbar's Gallery.* $500-1,500.

Chevrolet, GM's entry level division and biggest producer, passed Ford for the number 1 spot in 1927, as Ford sat dormant for six months while retooling to make the Model A. Propelling Chevrolet was its new Stovebolt Six motor, developed by engineer Ormond Hunt. The engine used cast-iron pistons (called the Cast-iron Wonder) and was as reliable as the Model T, and the car had a far more modern exterior design. It sold a million in 1927, priced at an affordable $595.

Chevrolet Motor Cars 1920 calendar, of Canada, 12" x 24". *Courtesy of Dunbar's Gallery.* $100-250.

Shortly after being ousted, for the first time, from GM, William Durant went to world-class racecar driver Louis Chevrolet and asked him to design a car. Durant wanted a car to rival the Model T. Chevrolet wanted a work of art more in keeping with his own standing. The result was the Classic Six, at $2,100 not a rival with Ford, but a good start. Within five years, not being able to work with Durant, Chevrolet left his namesake company. Durant made a million dollars in profits, which enabled him to snap up huge quantities of GM stock, in 1915 forcing a merger that put Durant back in the driver's seat of GM and gave GM the auto divisional lineup that it has to this day.

Chevrolet Super Service porcelain sign, with bow tie, circa 1950, double sided, 58" diameter. *Courtesy of Dunbar's Gallery.* $400-1,200.

In 1935, Chevrolet sold its ten millionth car; in 1939 the fifteen millionth car. Even though the Depression slashed overall sales and profits, Chevrolet rolled on. Unlike the Buick divison, Chevrolet always seemed to make the right decisions at the right time.

Chevrolet Genuine Parts enamel on steel flange sign, 18" x 18". *Courtesy of Dunbar's Gallery.* $200-700.

In the early 1930s, Chevrolet received a facelift. General Manager William Knudsen assigned Harley Earl to the division and the result was a series of elegant-looking cars at affordable prices. Harley Earl went on to become GM's chief designer through the '50s, the era of size and power.

Chevrolet GM Genuine Parts enamel on steel, double-sided hanging sign, circa 1950s, with logo, 18" x 24". *Courtesy of Dunbar's Gallery.* $150-450.

GM had a huge year in 1955, introducing V-8 engines in the "smaller," lower-priced lines such as Chevrolet, which boasted a 265 ci in its ultraclassic BelAir series. With the advent of an ambitious highway program and a nation's flight to the suburbs, speed was what the public wanted and got.

Chevrolet Dealership Poster, 1941, 48" x 18". *Courtesy of Dunbar's Gallery.* $100-300.

Another million-car year for Chevrolet in 1941, and it boasted of its dominance over Ford in this dealership poster. With GM's idea of planned obsolescence, i.e., making changes each year so that the car owner would be dissatisfied and would want a new car, insured that each year its cars would look new in some way, completely the opposite thinking of Henry Ford.

Oldsmobile Service pre-war double-sided porcelain sign, early logo in center, 42" diameter. *Courtesy of Dunbar's Gallery.* $500-1,000.

Like most entrepreneurs, Ransom E. Olds was his own man. Originally an engine maker in the late 1800s, he built the first production car in the United States, the curved-dash Olds, in 1901, and it did so well in just a few years that songs were written for his car and he sold out in 1904, retiring at forty. Soon, he decided to get back into the auto game and started his second company, which made REO's, a company he ran until he retired in 1924, a year that it had sales of $50 million.

OK neon, single-sided porcelain sign, 24" diameter. *Courtesy of Dunbar's Gallery.* $400-1,200.

The fallout of GM's idea of planned obsolescence was the used cars that were traded in for new. A whole new market was built selling "OK" used cars to those who couldn't, or didn't want to spring for the latest and greatest offerings from Detroit.

Oldsmobile porcelain sign, double sided, Rocket "88" Globe/Saturn Logo. *Courtesy of Dunbar's Gallery.* $200-800.

William Durant acquired Oldsmobile in 1909 as part of his General Motors lineup. A more expensive car than Chevrolet and Pontiac, Oldsmobile became GM's technical leader, as it was the first to offer the option of the automatic "Hydramatic" transmission in 1937. It used four speeds and added $57 to the price of the car. After World War II, Cadillac and Pontiac also went hydramatic, follwed by Nash, Hudson, and Kaiser-Frazer in the 1950s.

OK Chevrolet used cars porcelain sign, 18" diameter. *Courtesy of Dunbar's Gallery.* $100-400.

Quality OK Used Cars on one side, "Value You Can Trust" on the other, enamel on steel sign, 50s, 16" x 28". *Courtesy of Dunbar's Gallery.* $100-350.

Signs tried to inbue confidence in prospective used car buyers, even if salesmen didn't.

OAKLAND

SALES - SERVICE

PONTIAC

Oakland Pontiac Sales-Service porcelain sign, double sided, 1920s, 35-1/2" x 24" *Courtesy of Dunbar's Gallery.* $200-600.

Oakland, founded in 1907 in Pontiac, Michigan, and acquired by GM in 1909, was one of GM's few divisions that didn't make it to the present. A average-priced car, it enjoyed moderate success into the mid-1920s, when introduction of Pontiac caused Oakland sales to drop so much that after 1931 only Pontiacs were made.

Pontiac Chief weathervane, circa 1920s, 50"
x 49-1/2", on gallery stand. *Courtesy of
Dunbar's Gallery.* $300-1,000.

*Pontiac was introduced at the
height of the roaring '20s, in 1926, as
part of the Oakland division. However,
it sold so many models in its inception
(140,000 the first year) that GM
dropped the Oakland name by the early
'30s, Pontiac was the sandwich model
between Chevrolet and Oldsmobile.
During the Depression, GM combined
these manufacturing facilities to
consolidate resources.*

Pontiac Indian head
figural showroom display,
wire, circa 1930, 47" x
20". *Courtesy of
Dunbar's Gallery.* $200-
600.

*Pontiac, the last in
the GM nameplate line,
also offers the most
distinctive logo.*

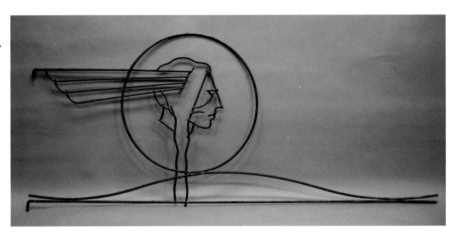

Pontiac Indian head figural porcelain sign, 50" x 35", circa 1940s. *Courtesy
of Dunbar's Gallery.* $300-800.

*The Pontiac logo inspired model names such as Chieftain and
Star Chief for its mid-1950s series.*

Pontiac 1949 calendar featuring embossed
iridescent Indian, full calendar, 20" x 32".
Courtesy of Dunbar's Gallery. $100-250.

*In 1949, the new Streamliner body
style was offered, one of super designer
Harley Earl's creations and a new high-
compression head boosted horsepower.*

Pontiac Sales-Service porcelain sign, framed, circa 1930s, 51" x 28". *Courtesy of Dunbar's Gallery.* $500-1,500.

Even though it was the last name on the GM marquee, Pontiac has consistently maintained high sales for the company, spending most of the last seventy years in the top five.

Pontiac Authorized Service porcelain sign, circa 1930s, 42" diameter. *Courtesy of Dunbar's Gallery.* $200-700.

In 1964, Pontiac built what's known as the first muscle car, the Pontiac Tempest GTO coupe, with a 389hp V8, which could outrun all the expensive sports cars at a fraction of the cost.

Pontiac Goodwill Porcelain Sign, 36" x 36". *Courtesy of Dunbar's Gallery.* $200-700.

In the 1950s Pontiac offered value in pricing and switched to V8s, culminating with the Bonneville, Chief, and Chieftain series.

United Motors Service double-sided porcelain/neon sign, Walker & Co., 46" x 28". *Courtesy of Dunbar's Gallery.* $500-2,000.

United Motors was an associated, sister company of General Motors that did not actually produce cars but offered a number of related auto services and products. Its distinctive open-auto logo makes this series of signs highly collectible.

United Motors Service neon/porcelain sign, circa 1920s, 24" diameter. *Courtesy of Dunbar's Gallery.* $500-1,500.

Signs were made in a variety of sizes, for both indoor and outdoor use.

United Motors oval porcelain sign, two sided, circa 1930, 48" x 28". *Courtesy of Dunbar's Gallery.* $300-900.

Chrysler Plymouth Sales & Service porcelain sign, double sided, circa 1930s, 35" x 18". *Courtesy of Dunbar's Gallery.* $200-700.

Walter Chrysler was a railroad man who fell in love with cars at his first auto show. He signed on with the Buick division of GM in 1911. By 1914 he had upped production of Buicks from forty-five cars a day to 560. After a falling out with GM president Durant in 1920, he left the company, took over Maxwell-Chalmers, and began producing his own car, the six-cylinder Chrysler '70', in 1924, selling $5 million worth the first year alone. He bought Dodge for $175 million in 1928, helping him become the third member of the "Big 3" car makers in Detroit. That year Chrysler also developed the four-cylinder Plymouth line to compete with Ford and Chevy. Chrysler's other legacy is the Chrysler Building, which he financed and built in the 1930s, second in size only to the Empire State Building.

United Motors Service figural porcelain sign, 17" x 18". *Courtesy of Dunbar's Gallery.* $500-1,500.

One of the smallest United Motors Service signs offered, it is desirable for the early service companies listed on the hanging signs and also for its size.

DODGE BROTHERS APPROVED SERVICE STATION

Dodge Brothers Approved Service Station porcelain sign, double sided, circa 1920s, 40" x 20". *Courtesy of Dunbar's Gallery.* Scarce and early, $200-600.

    John and Horace Dodge were part of the infancy of the automobile, supplying transmissions to early Olds, engine builders and shareholders of the fledgling Ford Co. The brothers opened their own business in Detroit in 1914 and were among the first to perform auto safety tests. Their early four-cylinder cars were used in World War I because they were tough and dependable. The public also thought so—Dodge rose to fourth in U.S. sales in 1916 and moved to second by 1920. The brothers were fine engineers and tough negotiators, often using the good cop/bad cop method. They also were big drinkers who like to work hard and play hard. Close throughout their lives, they also suffered from bad luck and, at the pinnacle of their success, died during the influenza epidemic of 1918-1920. The company was taken over by a New York bank until Chrysler purchased it from their widows in 1928, and the 70-year-old Chrysler-Dodge alliance was born.

Dodge-Plymouth round thermometer, glass face, Pam Clock Co., circa 1940, Bob Hess, Inc. 13" diameter. *Courtesy of Dunbar's Gallery.* $200-500, scarce.

    By the late 1930s-40s, Dodge styling was hard to distinguish from its cousins, DeSotos and Plymouths.

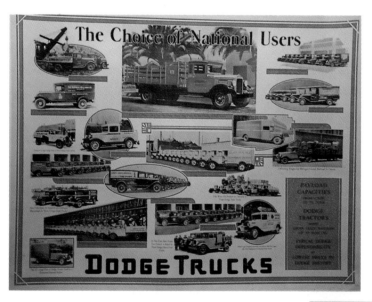

Dodge Trucks poster aimed at the commercial market, circa late 1920s, 45" x 36". *Courtesy of Dunbar's Gallery.* $100-300.

    Like other members of the Big 3, Dodge found a lucrative and constant market in commercial vehicles.

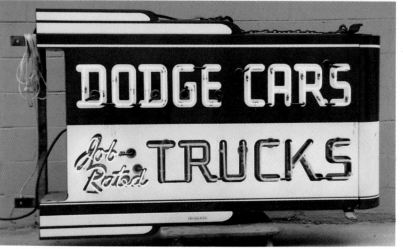

Dodge Job Rated Trucks, double-sided, neon, porcelain sign, Walker & Co., circa 1930s, 73" x 45" x 17". *Courtesy of Dunbar's Gallery.* $1,000-3,500.

    In the early 1930s, Dodge maintained a separate look and identity from Chrysler and Plymouth, although a bit of airflow styling spilled over, and their share of the market, with models priced from $700-1,700.

19

Dodge Plymouth diecut porcelain shield, 48" x 23". *Courtesy of Dunbar's Gallery.* $200-500.

Averaging 100,000 cars sold a year during the Depression, Dodge maintained its number-four position in sales with models that gave value and durability with conservative styling. With the failure of the more radical Chrysler and DeSoto Airflow models to capture America's imagination, it was left to Dodge sales to keep the cash flowing.

Mopar DeSoto Dodge Parts tin flange sign, circa 1950s, 24" x 15". *Courtesy of Dunbar's Gallery.* $100-350.

In the mid-1950s, Dodge underwent a transformation. First, the Red Ram V8 was dropped in. Then Virgil Exner, formerly of Studebaker, came over and revamped Dodge's whole look, turning out a whole new Royal series that would compete with the Chevy Bel Air.

Hudson-Essex Service porcelain sign, double sided, 30" x 16". *Courtesy of Dunbar's Gallery.* $100-450.

This large independent maker started in 1909 and made a reputation for an upscale auto with some hefty pep under the hood. The 1920s were a heyday for Hudson, partially thanks to sales of Essex, its less expensive line. Like other companies, Hudson contributed to the war effort, turning over its factory to military production. In the 1950s, the company fortunes faltered. Hudson merged with Nash to create American Motors in 1954, but the name was gone by 1958 as the Big 3 (GM, Ford, Chrysler) pushed out most of the independents by the late 50s. GM, in particular, blitzed America with television and print advertising. The result was a brand identification so popular that the smaller companies consistently lost sales to GM in the '50s. Most companies spent the 1950s merging and consolidating to compete. By 1964, almost all of these companies were gone, and others, reorganized again, were barely hanging on. The Big 3 was winning the monopoly game.

Hudson Sales and Service Station porcelain sign, double sided, circa 1930s, 23" x 20". *Bob & Judy Palmerino Collection, Courtesy of Noel Barrett Auctions.* Rare, $600-2,000.

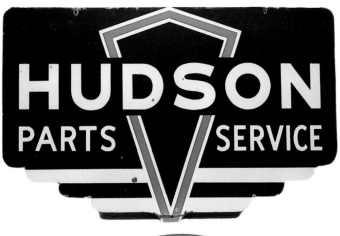

Hudson porcelain sign, 42" x 26", double sided. *Courtesy of Dunbar's Gallery.* $200-600.

The late '40s were good to Hudson. In 1948, they built a brand new Step-Down series with a high compression L-head motor, as the Big 3 were behind in getting their new designs to the public. Sales hit 145,000 in 1950, Hudson's post-World War II pinnacle.

Rambler Parts Service porcelain sign, double sided, 42" diameter. *Courtesy of Dunbar's Gallery.* $200-450.

Rambler made its reappearance after World War I (it was first made by the Jeffrey Co. in the teens before being bought by Nash). It developed into Nash's dependable and inexpensive line. After Nash and Hudson combined to form American Motors in 1954, the Rambler brand lived on while AMC dropped both the Hudson and Nash lines.

Nash Service Parts diecut shield porcelain sign, double sided, 46" x 46". *Courtesy of Dunbar's Gallery.* $200-700.

When William Durant took over GM for the second time in 1915, president Charles Nash was one of the first casualties, as he and Durant did not get along. In 1916, Nash bought the Thomas B. Jeffrey Co. of Kenosha, Wisconsin and began selling Nashes under his own name in 1918. During the 1920s he acquired Mitchell and Lafayette. Like many of the larger companies, Nash developed lines to appeal to those looking for transportation and those looking for luxury. He loved gadgets. In the 1930s, innovations included a dashboard starter button, cowl vents, shatterproof glass, combination ignition and steering locks, and aircraft-style instruments. The company squeezed through the Depression and World War II, being the first dealer to offer air conditioning as an option in 1939. Enjoying postwar success, Nash offered a new model called the Airflyte, which helped boost them into the top ten in production in 1949. In early 1950s, they brought out their tiny sports car convertible, based on the Fiat, called the Metropolitan, which has a cult following today. Like most of the independents, in the mid-50s Nash had to merge to compete with the Big Three and became American Motors Company in 1954. By 1957, the Nash name was gone, another nameplate in the boneyard.

Kaiser/Willys Approved Service porcelain sign, double sided, 42" diameter. *Courtesy of Dunbar's Gallery.* $200-600.

Kaiser joined with Willys in 1953, concentrating on Jeep sales until their sale to Dodge in the 1980s.

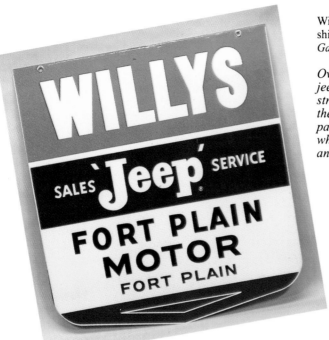

Willys Jeep double-sided, enamel on steel, shield sign, 24" x 26". *Courtesy of Dunbar's Gallery.* $100-400.

Jeep made its mark in World War II. Overland Willys produced 660,000 jeeps, which symbolized America's strength and tenacity. Fifty years later, the sport utility market is thriving, particularly among young professionals who like the capability of driving over and/or through any conditions.

Thurston the magician litho on cardboard display, circa late 1920s. 31" x 45", framed. *Courtesy of Dunbar's Gallery.* $500-1,500.

Whippets were made under the Overland name in the late 1920s, then briefly under the Willys name until their discontinuation in 1931. Overland was founded in 1903. Because of financial problems, John Willys bought into the company and renamed it Willys-Overland. An independent, this company made cars for years. Its greatest contribution, however, is the Jeep, which it sold for civilian use after World War II.

Ford porcelain sign, Veribrite, circa 1930, framed, 40" x 26". *Courtesy of Dunbar's Gallery.* Scarce, $300-1,500.

In 1896, while working for the Detroit Edison Illuminating Co., Henry Ford built his first car, at the age of 32, the "quadricycle," with a two-cylinder engine. In 1902 he put together the financial backing to start his own company and produced the first Ford Model A in 1903, at $850. By 1906 he was at the top, a spot Ford would hold until 1927, helped by the Model T, introduced in 1908. Ford also developed the method of assembly-line production (originally thought of by Ransom E. Olds) in 1913, which increased the amount of cars put together each day while decreasing costs, which Ford passed on to his customers. By 1920, more than two million cars were sold in the US, and a million of them were Fords.

Genuine Ford Parts porcelain sign, double sided, stamped "Veribrite" and "Property of Ford Motor Co.," 23" x 16". *Courtesy of Dunbar's Gallery.* $100-500.

This sign has been reproduced. The easiest way to tell an original is to make sure it has been stamped "Property of Ford Motor Company" on the very bottom margin of the sign, like this one.

Buick and Ford cars repair figural tin sign, 1920s, Eugene Thomas Garage, 12" x 35". *Courtesy of Dunbar's Gallery.* $100-300.

If Henry Ford saw this sign, he probably would have ripped it down. In his mind, Ford was the only car for the masses and the only one needed. His son, Edsel, was more far sighted and even tempered, but, after battling with his father for years, he succumbed to stomach cancer in 1943. His father lived for several more years, seeing his grandson, Henry II, take over the company in 1946.

Lincoln Ford Fordson lightup wooden sign, circa 1920s, 72" x 18". *Courtesy of Dunbar's Gallery.* Rare, $500-3,000.

Ford ruled the automobile empire in the teens and 1920s. While other companies produced models for all pocketbooks and tastes, Henry Ford insisted on only the Model T and only in black, because black paint took the least time to dry. The Model T was reliable for getting from point A to point B, and, for a long time that was accepted by the public, with more than 15 million "Tin Lizzies" sold in its nineteen-year run. However, the 1920s were the era of jazz, speakeasys, new money, and hot style. With the inroads made in body design and engineering by other companies, by the late 1920s the Model T looked as outdated as a corset to a flapper. Sales slumped and Ford was forced to close his factory for six months and quickly create a new car, which he did—the Model A. Witholding all details and photos about the new car created a frenzy, and Ford was swamped with 450,000 orders in the first two weeks alone.

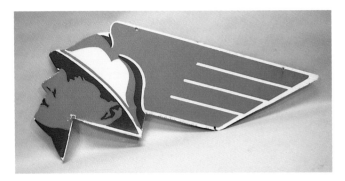

Mercury figural diecut porcelain sign, double sided, circa 1939, 30" x 15". *Courtesy of Dunbar's Gallery.* $400-1,000.

Created in 1938, this model was made to compete with Oldsmobile and Buick, and has done so for sixty years.

Ford Service Entrance sign, 42" x 10". *Courtesy of Dunbar's Gallery.* $100-250.

In 1914, Henry Ford doubled wages of assembly line workers, from $2.30 to $5 a day, so his own workers could afford a Model T, now priced at $440 and dropping. People poured in from all parts of the country to try to get a job. Previous assembly line turnover was more than 400 percent a year. The new wage knocked it down to 37 percent at Ford. However, Ford was also the last to succumb to unionization in the 1930s, instead hiring a former boxer and sailor, Harry Bennett, to head the Ford Service Department, which provided nothing but fear and violence. Bennett was a thug whose gang terrified workers, creating a horrendous working enviroment that probably helped the workers band together and strike back. One of Henry II's first acts as president was to fire Harry Bennett.

Ford Farming tin sign, 20" x 12". *Courtesy of Dunbar's Gallery.* $75-200.

Packard enamel on steel agency sign, circa 1950s, from Maggard Motor, Inc., North 7th St., Bozeman, Montana, 96" x 88". *Courtesy of Dunbar's Gallery.* $1,000-3,000.

This particular sign was supposed to hang from this building, but never made it out of the crate. Later it was used as a headboard. Packard, in its heyday before World War II, was the quintessential American car, packed with luxury and power. Founded in 1899 in Warren Ohio, the Packard brothers moved to Detroit to be close to the action. They made the world's first twelve-cylinder, the Twin Six, in 1915; a special racing version reached 149.9 mph at Daytona in 1919. Packard regularly put out more cars than Cadillac and in 1929 more people owned Packard stock than any other company except for GM. For $5,200-6,000, in the 1930s, you could buy a house or a Packard Speedster 8, of which only 150 were built.

Packard dealership double-sided porcelain sign, circa 1930, 60" diameter. *Courtesy of Dunbar's Gallery.* $1,000-2,500.

In 1935, Packard offered a less-expensive model for only $980, selling 24,000 of 31,000 total production. However, Packard continued to concentrate on its luxury Super 8 and Twelve models, driven by movie stars and executives who hadn't leapt from the 52nd floor.

Packard Authorized Service enamel on steel sign, double sided, 12" x 7". *Courtesy of Dunbar's Gallery.* $75-200.

Packard never regained its position after World War II. Postwar cars didn't have the same styling. To survive, the company merged with Studebaker and lasted until 1958.

Studebaker porcelain neon sign, circa 1930s, single sided, upper and lower sections, no tubing, Walker & Co., 12' x 31". *Courtesy of Dunbar's Gallery.* $300-1,000.

Studebaker first made its name in wagons, the leading maker for the second half of the nineteenth century. Only one of five brothers, John, lived to see Studebaker's first horseless carriage, an electric model, drive off in 1902. He ran the company until his death in 1917.

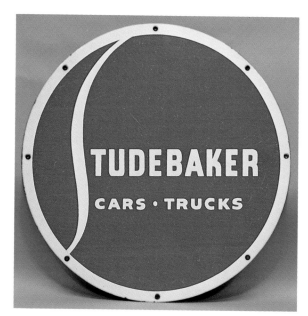

Studebaker Cars-Trucks porcelain sign, 20" diameter. *Courtesy of Dunbar's Gallery.* $100-700.

Postwar Studebakers offered distinctive design— lots of glass, flowing fenders, and a clean, low profile. As the '50s progressed, production and sales fell and Studebaker merged with Packard 1954. Just before Studebaker closed its doors n 1964, it created one more model, the Avanti, an exotic sports car sought by collectors today.

Russell Motor Cars, Distributors of Gardner Cars, wooden sign, double sided, 72" x 24", circa 1920s. *Bob & Judy Palmerino Collection, Courtesy of Noel Barrett Auctions.* Scarce, $300-1,000.

Gardner cars, from its inception of 1919 to 1931, ran with specially made Lycoming L-head engines in 4-8 cylinders. Based in St. Louis, the company showed an unusually low-slung front-wheel drive six at the 1930 New York Auto Show before fading into auto oblivion.

Studebaker neon sign, 26" diameter, 1930s, rare and fantastic. *Courtesy of Dunbar's Gallery.* $1,000-4,000.

The early '30s were mixed for the company. On the racetrack, Studebaker Presidents were winners. However, the company's own head, Albert Erskine Russell, made a series of bad decisions that forced the company into receivership. He resigned and soon after committed suicide. Studebaker lived on, as management concentrated on a small midrange which sold well up to World War II.

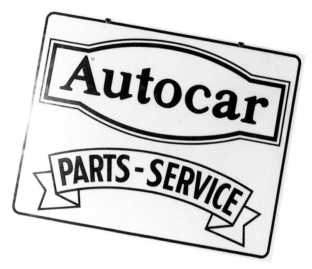

Studebaker Service porcelain sign, double sided, 20" x 24", circa 1920s. *Bob & Judy Palmerino Collection, Courtesy of Noel Barrett Auctions.* $500-1,500. Plymouth Service porcelain sign, circa 1930s, double sided, 18" x 22". *Bob & Judy Palmerino Collection, Courtesy of Noel Barrett Auctions.* $300-800.

Plymouth was former GM president Walter Chrysler's answer to Durant's GM Chevy, consistently rivaling both Ford and Chevy in sales.

Autocar Parts-Service porcelain sign, double sided, circa 1910, 36" x 28". *Bob & Judy Palmerino Collection, Courtesy of Noel Barrett Auctions.* Rare, $200-900.

This company began life in 1897, in Pittsburgh, Pennsylvania, and moved its facilities to Ardmore, Pennsylvania, in 1900. It produced mostly experimental models, including the first multi-cylinder shaft-driven car in America. The company introduced a truck line in 1907, making only trucks after 1911, and is now a division of White Motor Co., making heavy trucks.

Chalmers Motor Cars porcelain sign, circa 1915, 71" x 24". *Bob & Judy Palmerino Collection, Courtesy of Noel Barrett Auctions.* Scarce, $400-1,200.

Hugh Chalmers, vice-president of National Cash Register Co., took over the Thomas-Detroit company in 1907, changing the name of the game. By 1915, the company was making 20,000 cars a year. Although a relatively short-lived company, Chalmers of Detroit sold well in the United States for a decade, also distinguishing itself on the racetrack in the early 1900s. After World War I, sales waned. Chalmers merged with Maxwell and then both were acquired by Walter Chrysler in the early 1920s.

Marmon-Roosevelt Authorized Service porcelain sign, double sided, 30î w x 24î h, circa 1929-1930. *Bob & Judy Palmerino Collection, Courtesy of Noel Barrett Auctions.* Very rare, $1,000-2,500.

The Roosevelt, named for Teddy, was brought out for only two years, an affordable straight-8 costing under $1,000, which was completely against the company's (and former president's image. Marmon was founded in Indianapolis in 1902. In the early years, Marmons were fast, taking fifty-four first-place finishes between 1909 and 1912, and winning the first Indianapolis 500 in 1911. Marmons were also a car for the wealthy, costing over $5,000 in the 1920s. The crowning achievement was a Marmon Sixteen, in 1931. However, management and sales' squabbles over direction and the Depression combined to close down the company by the mid 1930s.

Flint Authorized Service porcelain sign, double sided, 30" x 20", circa 1920s. *Bob & Judy Palmerino Collection, Courtesy of Noel Barrett Auctions.* $400-1,000.

Owned by the Locomobilie Co., Flint was built with a Continental six-cylinder engine and sold in the $2,000 range. It survived until 1927.

Gas and Oil Signs, Posters

Estes & Co's Garage silk-screened tin sign, circa 1910-20, 12" x 35" *Courtesy of Dunbar's Gallery.* Scarce, $300-700.

Early signs were silk screened on tin and made individually by stations until the late teens to early 1920s.

Penn-Drake Motor Oil porcelain sign, double sided, picturing the first oil well in the United States, 21" x 27". *Bob & Judy Palmerino Collection, Courtesy of Noel Barrett Auctions.* $400-1,000.

The first commercial oil well in the United States was drilled by salt miner William Smith in Titusville, Pennsylvania. Edwin Drake oversaw the drilling. He later opted out of drilling for the oil stock market, which left him penniless. However, his name lived in the Penn-Drake brand.

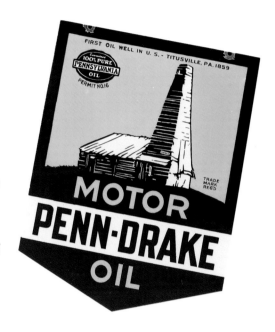

Texaco Motoroil double-sided porcelain sign, 42", diameter, later version of the filling station sign, circa 1920s. *Courtesy of Dunbar's Gallery.* $350-1,200.

Texaco, organized in 1903 in Sour Lake, Texas, was the first complete company that ran all its own operations, from production and refining to distribution.

Texaco "Filling Station" double-sided porcelain sign, 42" diameter, 1915, earliest porcelain gasoline station sign with national logo. *Courtesy Dunbar Moonlight Kid Auctions.* $1,000-3,000.

To stand out from the hardware and general stores offering curbside gas, the burgeoning national companies had to distinguish themselves. In placing logo signs in front of their own pumps, patrons could feel confident in the quality of their product, if not always the honesty of the pumper.

Texaco Easy Pour Can enamel on steel flange sign, circa 1920, 27" x 17". *Bob & Judy Palmerino Collection, Courtesy of Noel Barrett Auctions.* $1,000-2,000.

    The gloved hand lends a nice touch.

Texaco Easy Pour Can porcelain sign, circa 1920, 24" x 24". *Courtesy of Dunbar's Gallery.*

    Before finally settling on the one-quart can as the uniform container, manufacturers tried a variety of amounts, including two quarts, up to 5- and 10-gallon containers.

Clean, Clear, Golden Texaco Motor Oil porcelain sign, circa 1930s, 12" x 14". *Courtesy of Dunbar's Gallery.* $200-600.

    One of the most aggressive companies, Texaco, once established, added drilling sites in Wichita Falls, Electra, and Petrolia, supplying East Coast refineries with more crude oil in one year than Pennsylvania had in the previous ten.

Texaco Motor Oil Ford porcelain sign, 15" x 5". *Courtesy of Dunbar's Gallery.* $150-300.

    As fortunes of one related to the fortunes of the other, auto companies and oil companies worked together for their mutual benefit.

Texaco with pouring oil insert, single-sided porcelain sign, "Free Crank Case Service," 30" x 30". *Courtesy of Dunbar Moonlight Kid Auctions.* $200-500.

As gas stations have not always have the best reputation for cleanliness and quality, the large companies made sure to use just those images to inspire confidence and loyalty in their customers.

Oilzum Motor Oil tin upright sign, circa 1920s, 12" x 60". *Courtesy of Dunbar's Gallery.* $200-800.

Oilzum used a black, white, or orange background throughout the 1920s.

Oilzum embossed brass sign, circa 1910-15, 80" x 20". *Courtesy of Dunbar's Gallery.* $500-5,000.

White & Bagley was founded in Worcester, Massachusetts, as a lubricants manufacturer. Their first motor oil was introduced in 1906. Their second and most enduring logo was that of Oswald, a.k.a. the Oilzum Man, with trademark cap and goggles.

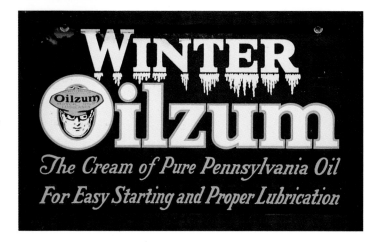

Oilzum "Winter" tin sign, circa 1947, 22" x 13-1/2". *Courtesy of Dunbar's Gallery.* $200-400.

In the late 1940s, Oilzum went to a green background.

Oilzum tin sign, with Oilzum Man logo, 1940s, 72" x 36". *Courtesy of Dunbar's Gallery.* $200-700.

This is one of the best advertising slogans, ever.

Oilzum Motor Oil tin sign, 1958, 36" x 17". *Courtesy of Dunbar's Gallery.* $100-350.

The Oilzum man lived until 1988, when the company merged with the Dryden Oil Co. of Baltimore, Maryland.

Oilzum Motor Oil tin thermometer, 1950s, 7-1/2" x 15". *Courtesy of Dunbar's Gallery.* $100-500.

Oilzum Motor Oil enamel on steel sign, 29" x 32". *Courtesy of Dunbar's Gallery.* $100-400.

Oilzum auto racing poster, 1939, Wilbur Shaw winner of Indy 500 using Oilzum, testimonial by Cotton Henning, pre-war black and orange logo, 17" x 24". *Courtesy of Dunbar Moonlight Kid Auctions.* $200-500.

Advertising hasn't changed very much since its inception. Testimonials are still popular. Looking at race cars today, it's hard to see the metal under a covering of ads for everything from Mellow Yellow to 7-11.

Oilzum auto racing poster 1940, Wilbur Shaw Winner Indy 500 using Oilzum, titled "Another Victory," testimonial by Cotton Henning, 17" x 24". *Courtesy of Dunbar Moonlight Kid Auctions.* $200-500.

Oilzum auto racing poster, 1946, George Robson winner Indy 500 using Oilzum, 17" x 24". The first Indy following World War II. *Courtesy of Dunbar Moonlight Kid Auctions.* $100-400.

Oilzum auto racing poster 1947 "Racing Victories," National AAA Champ Ted Horn, list of drivers and races won using Oilzum: Mauri Rose, Bill Holland, Tony Bettenhauser, 17" x 24". *Courtesy of Dunbar Moonlight Kid Auctions.* $100-400.

General Gasoline porcelain sign, double sided, circa 1920s, 30" diameter. *Bob & Judy Palmerino Collection, Courtesy of Noel Barrett Auctions.* $300-1,000.
General Petroleum Corp. was found in 1910 in Vernon, California. The company was bought by Socony in 1926, keeping the name alive until 1936, when the products were replaced by Mobilgas.

Mobil porcelain Pegasus, circa 1930s, with brackets, embossed-style outline, 52" long. *Courtesy of Dunbar's Gallery.* $500-1,500.

The Mobil Pegasus is, arguably, the best known and best loved oil/gas company logo. The Socony and Vacuum (makers of Mobil) companies merged in 1931 and soon after adopted the Socony Pegasus as the official Mobil mascot.

Mobil porcelain Pegasus, circa 1930s, with brackets, flat version, 52" long. *Courtesy of Dunbar's Gallery.* $500-1,500.

When looking at a Pegasus to buy, make sure it has the mounting brackets on the rear side. Reproductions won't. Also, note that these horses come in sizes 2-4 feet long.

Mobiloil Gargoyle tin upright sign, single sided, 15" x 60". *Courtesy of Dunbar's Gallery.* $200-800.

Mobil started life as the Vacuum Oil Co. of Rochester, New York, founded as a lubicants manufacturer in 1866. Standard Oil purchased the company in 1879 until the Standard monopoly breakup of 1911, when Vacuum once again became an independent company. The Gargoyle logo was first used to sell Mobiloil, then, in the late 1920s, Mobilgas. After Socony and Vaccum merged in 1931, the gargoyle was replaced by the Pegasus.

Mobiloil Gargoyle tin cabinet sign, 1920s, embossed, single sided, 13-1/2" x 17". *Courtesy of Dunbar's Gallery.* $150-450.

Socony Motor Oils porcelain sign, circa 1920s, 36" x 18". *Courtesy of Dunbar's Gallery*. $200-500.

Socony (Standard Oil Co. of New York) was originally the administrative division of the Standard Oil Trust, broken up in 1911. Socony marketed its own products through its own name and then acquired the Magnolia Petroleum Co. in 1918 and the General Petroleum Co. in 1926. After merging with the Vacuum Co. in 1931, it marketed its products primarily under the Mobil name and in 1966 was renamed the Mobil Corp.

Socony Air-Craft Oils porcelain sign, single sided, 1925-31, 30" x 20". *Courtesy of Dunbar's Gallery*. $500-1,500.

A personal note: When my father, who has always worked in the car business, met my mother, he misspelled hers name "Socony," until she corrected him—she's Ciccone of Italy, not Socony of New York. Being a pilot, and with the name mixup, this has always been her favorite sign.

Magnolia Petroleum Co. "Gas for Sale Here" porcelain curb sign, with magnolia logo, circa 1918-1925, 30" diameter. *Courtesy of Dunbar's Gallery*. $200-900.

Magnolia, from Dallas, Texas, produced oils and gas from 1911, selling 45 percent interest to Socony in 1918. Socony bought out the company completely in 1925. The brand name was replaced by Mobilgas in 1934, but Magnolia remained a subsidiary in pipeline transportation until 1960.

Magnolia porcelain sign, with Mobil Pegasus, dated 1956, unusual, 27" x 16". Probably some type of pipeline sign used. *Courtesy of Dunbar's Gallery*. $200-600.

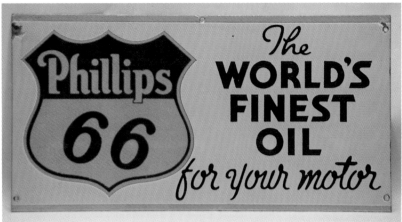

Phillips 66 double-sided porcelain sign, 1936-1940, 22" x 11". *Courtesy of Dunbar's Gallery.* $300-900.

Phillips started as a refiner and producer in Bartlesville, Oklahoma, in 1917. It wasn't until 1927 that the company opened its first gasoline station in Witchita, Kansas. Spreading faster than a careless match, the company had 6,000 stations by 1930.

Red Crown gasoline porcelain sign, 42" diameter, early, with a couple of factory blemishes and edge chips. *Courtesy of Dunbar's Gallery.* $500-1,000.

Phillips 66 double-sided figural shield porcelain sign, 48" x 47", 1930s-1940s. *Courtesy of Dunbar's Gallery.* $200-600.

To make its logo distinctive yet familiar, Phillips chose the shield form used for highway route designations.

Red Crown gasoline with Polarine upright thermometer and porcelain sign, without writing in crown, 18" x 72". *Courtesy of Dunbar's Gallery.* $700-2,000.

Red Hat Motor Oil enamel on steel flange sign, circa 1925-1929, 18" diameter with 1-1/2" flange. *Courtesy of Dunbar's Gallery.* Scarce, $500-2,000.

The Independent Oil Men of America, IOMA, formed in 1925 to organize independent gas/oil marketers and give them a voice against the major companies with more money and clout. To ensure quality, they chose the Red Hat trademark. Unfortunately, Standard Oil, maker of Red Crown, sued and won, forcing IOMA to change its logo. Therefore, Red Hat signs were short lived and are rare today.

Gulf porcelain sign, circa 1930s, 36" diameter.
Courtesy of Dunbar's Gallery. $200-500.

   *Gulf Oil Co. is now owned by Chevron,
which bailed out the company in the early
1980s. Gulf was founded in 1901 in Texas,
then moved operations to Pittsburgh, Pennsylvania, opening the nation's first drive-in gas
station in 1913 in that city. Most of the
stations were built in the south and east,
including Gulf's first retail station in Pittsburgh, in 1913.*

Gulf Supreme Auto Oil porcelain flange sign, 1920-22, Ingraham
Richardson, 21" x 17" x 1-1/2". *Courtesy of Dunbar's Gallery.*
$200-800.

   *Like most of the other large companies (Texaco,
Mobil, etc.) Gulf gobbled up regional companies to build
its station chain across the country in the 1950s.*

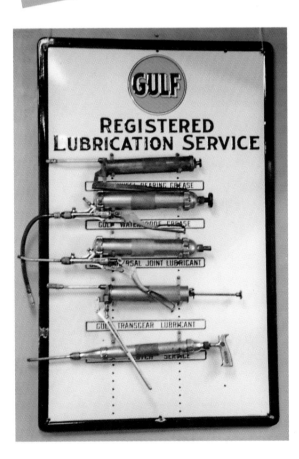

Gulf Registered Lubrication Service porcelain grease
gun display, circa 1930s, with five guns, porcelain
plates, stamped Ingraham Richardson, 30" x 48".
Courtesy of Dunbar's Gallery. $300-1,000.

   *The Depression slowed down the motoring
public as many people faced a constant choice of
gas or food. Many small companies went out of
business. To survive, the larger gas/oil companies
compensated with a variety of products and
services to make up for slumping gas sales.*

Gulf Authorized Dealer porcelain sign, circa 1920s,
40" x 9". *Courtesy of Dunbar's Gallery.* $200-600.

   *One of Gulf's earliest signs. Words like
"authorized" and "certified" were used to give
customers faith in the quality of the products sold.
Of course, we don't know who was doing the
authorizing and the certifying.*

Shell Motor Oil figural porcelain sign, double sided, circa 1920s, 25" x 25", unusual size. *Courtesy of Dunbar's Gallery.* $400-1,000.

Shell Oil Co., originally of England, first entered the American oil game in 1912, then purchased Roxana Petroleum in 1917, and sold petroleum products in all 48 states by 1929.

Shell diecut porcelain sign, 1930s, 42" x 42". *Courtesy of Dunbar's Gallery.* $500-1,500.

Veedol/Tydol "For Your Protection" double-sided tin sign, circa 1930s, 22" x 12". *Courtesy of Dunbar's Gallery.* $100-350.

The father company of Tydol and Veedol, Tidewater Oil Co., was founded in New York in 1887 and entered the gas market in 1915 using the Tydol name.

Flying A figural diecut porcelain sign, 65" x 27-1/2". *Courtesy of Dunbar Moonlight Kid Auctions.* Scarce $500-2,000.

After the merger between Tidewater and Associated in 1938, stations in the West became Associated Flying A stations and stations in the East were Tydol Flying A stations.

Veedol Tractor Oil wooden thermometer, 5" x 20". *Courtesy of Dunbar's Gallery.* $100-250.

Like many of the gas/ oil companies, Tidewater was always searching for new markets outside of automobiles. Related markets, such as aviation, farm equipment, and commercial trucks all needed attention and the company was only too happy to provide it.

Tydol Gasoline double-sided porcelain sign, circa 1930s, 42" diameter. *Courtesy of Dunbar's Gallery.* $300-600.

Tydol gas pricers, enamel on steel, circa 1920s, embossed, "15 to 25" on one side, "25 to 33" on the other, HD Beach Co., 13" x 8". *Courtesy of Dunbar's Gallery.* Scarce, $200-600.

New oil wells drilled in the 1920s created an unexpected gas glut, which found stations scrambling to cut prices to stay in competition. Different octanes also cost varying amounts, all of which is why stations needed changeable price signs.

Sinclair Opaline Motor Oil porcelain sign, 1930s, 48" x 20". *Courtesy of Dunbar's Gallery.* $300-1,000.

Today Sinclair is an idependent oil refiner and marketer that has stations in almost half of the United States.

Right: Sinclair Pennsylvania Motor Oil single sided porcelain sign, circa 1930s, 15" x 60". *Courtesy of Dunbar's Gallery.* $200-600.

Like Texaco, Sinclair started off as a completely integrated business, handling petroleum products from drilling to refining to marketing. Harry Sinclair founded the company in 1916 in New York, which prospered in the 1920s, despite his involvement with the Teapot Dome Oil Scandal.

American Oil Co. (Amoco) Authorized Station porcelain sign, circa 1920-26, 20" x 17". *Courtesy of Dunbar's Gallery.* $300-900.

American Oil Co. got its start in Baltimore in 1910, refining and marketing kerosene and introducing "Amoco-Gas" in 1915. In 1923, they signed an agreement with Pan American Petroleum of New Orleans, giving 50 percent of Amoco in exchange for the crude oil supply. In 1933, Pan-Am bought out Amoco. Then, in the food chain scenario, Standard of Indiana gobbled up Pan Am in 1954.

Greyhound Motor Fuel porcelain sign, 50" x 30". *Courtesy of Dunbar's Gallery.* Scarce, $200-800.

Texas Pacific Motor Oil porcelain sign, double sided, 1930s, 42" diameter. *Courtesy of Dunbar's Gallery.* Scarce, $500-2,000.

Texas Pacific Coal and Oil Co., of Fort Worth, Texas, was an independent marketer that was bought out by Humble (that was scooped up by Esso that was scooped up by Standard, one of the industry gluttons).

Esso Verified Lubrication porcelain sign, 21" x 6". *Courtesy of Dunbar's Gallery.* $100-350.

Besides "authorized" and "certified," "verified" is always a nice official word to inspire confidence in customers.

Esso "Credit Cards Honored" porcelain sign, circa '50s, double sided, 18" x 14". *Courtesy of Dunbar's Gallery.* $100-350.

Companies started using charge cards as early as the 1930s, as an extra incentive to inspire customer loyalty.

Pair of Esso extra porcelain pump signs, , Humble Oil Co., 15" x 20". *Courtesy of Dunbar's Gallery.* $100-500 each.

Esso, of Standard Oil of New Jersey, first came out at an Ethyl gasoline in 1926. Standard bought Humble in 1919. Esso expanded into nineteen states. In 1959, U.S. marketing was done under Humble as well as Esso. Signs like these are very hard to find, as Standard insisted on the return of their signs to corporate headquarters, and would then destroy the signs, creating an Esso sign shortage.

Richlube Motor Oil porcelain sign, double sided, circa early 1930s, 24" diameter. *Courtesy of Dunbar's Gallery.* $800-2,500.

Richfield has been primarily a West Coast company, founded in 1901, doing it all, producing, refining and marketing. However, the company created a subsidiary, Richfield of New York, and entered the East Coast markets, only to bow out again by selling the eastern marketing to Sinclair in the 1930s.

"Safety!" Richlube Motor Oil porcelain sign, double sided, 1930s, 24" diameter. *Courtesy of Dunbar's Gallery.* Rare, $1,000-3,500.
Also made by Richfield of New York.

Richfield Ethyl Gasoline porcelain sign, double sided, 1930s, 25", diameter. *Bob & Judy Palmerino Collection, Courtesy of Noel Barrett Auctions.* $900-2,200.

The ethyl additive was discovered to stop knocking in low-compression engines. This patent was purchased by the far-sighted GM conglomerate, which then entered into a partnership deal with Standard.

Power Lube Motor Oil porcelain sign, double sided, 28" x 20". *Courtesy of Dunbar Moonlight Kid Auctions.* $200-800.

A small quantity of these signs was found a number of years ago, almost all with condition problems on at least one side. This is one of the more dynamic logos.

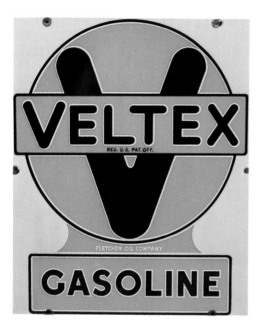

Veltex Gasoline porcelain sign, Fletcher Oil Co., circa 1940s, 18" x 24". *Courtesy of Dunbar's Gallery.* $200-600.
Fletcher, based in Boise, Idaho, still operates several stations in Idaho.

Silent Chief Gasoline porcelain sign, double sided, 40" diameter. *Bob & Judy Palmerino Collection, Courtesy of Noel Barrett Auctions.* One of two known, $5,000-10,000.

Republic porcelain station sign, red, shield logo, 48" x 52", circa 1930s. *Courtesy of Dunbar's Gallery.* $200-500.

Republic, of Pittsburgh, Pennsylvania, supplied jobbers in the southeast. It was bought out by Marathon in 1962 and the name was eventually phased out.

Pure Oil Steamship Co. sign, circa 1930s, 30" diameter. *Courtesy of Dunbar's Gallery.* Rare, $1,000-4,000.

Pure Oil began marketing gasoline from its location of Oil City, Pennsylvania, in 1914. In the 1920s Pure merged with a number of companies. It was company president Henry Dawes who gave architect C. A. Petersen a chance to design a distinctive service station. He did, creating the "cottage style," a homey building with sloped English roof that passed the beautification standards adopted by many towns in the 1930s after a seige of ugly, rundown stations threatened each municipality's aesthetics. Other companies fell in line quickly to create unique and attractive stations.

Pennzoil Motor Oil tin sign, can shaped, 32" x 47". *Courtesy of Dunbar's Gallery.* $100-450.

Amalie Motor Oil double-sided porcelain sign, dated 1933, 30" x 20". *Courtesy of Dunbar's Gallery.* $200-500.

41

Valvoline Racing Oil enamel on steel sign, double sided, 30 diameter, circa late 1950s. *Courtesy of Dunbar's Gallery.* $100-400.

    Valvoline is the oldest trademark in the petroleum industry today, introduced in 1873. Valvoline began marketing gasoline in the 1920s until it merged with the Freedom Oil Co. in 1944. After that, Valvoline went back to oil sales. It then merged with Ashland in 1950 and continues to be sold all over the world.

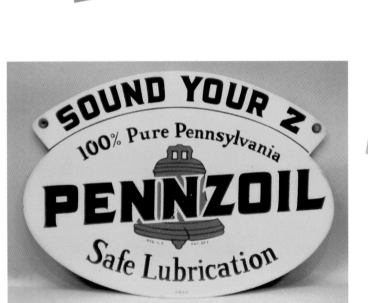

William Penn enamel on steel double-sided sign, 1949, 26" x 28". *Courtesy of Dunbar's Gallery.* $150-500.

Pennzoil tin sign, double sided, circa 1958, 16" x 12". *Courtesy of Dunbar's Gallery.* $50-175.

Pennzoil enamel on steel oval sign, 31" x 14". *Courtesy of Dunbar's Gallery.* $50-150.

    Pennzoil, of Houston, Texas, and Oil City, Pennsylvania, opened its first chain of stations in 1921. Its gas can still be found today in ten states, and its oil is sold all over the world.

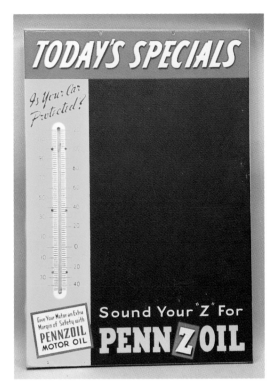

Pennzoil (Could someone explain "Sound Your Z" to me?) tin sign, 11" x 59". *Courtesy of Dunbar's Gallery.* Unusual, $100-450.

Pennzoil blackboard thermometer enamel on steel sign, 18-1/2" x 26-1/2". *Courtesy of Dunbar's Gallery.* $100-350.

Oriental Special Auto Oil porcelain sign, single sided, only example known, 17" x 21". *Bob & Judy Palmerino Collection, Courtesy of Noel Barrett Auctions.* $1,000-3,500.

Jenney Lubrication Service porcelain wall rack, 35" x 70". *Bob & Judy Palmerino Collection, Courtesy of Noel Barrett Auctions.* Rare, $500-1,500.

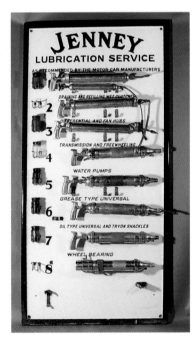

Jenney Gasoline porcelain sign, circa 1930s, 60" x 36", Boston, Massachussets. *Bob & Judy Palmerino Collection, Courtesy of Noel Barrett Auctions.* $100-600.

 Jenney Mfg. Co. originally dealt in whale oils and kerosene. It entered the gasoline market in the early 1900s. Best known in New England, Jenney merged with Cities Service in 1965 as Citgo.

Cities Service Gasoline and Motor Oils porcelain sign, double sided, circa 1920s, 60" x 36". *Bob & Judy Palmerino Collection, Courtesy of Noel Barrett Auctions.* Rare, $300-1,200.

 Based in Tulsa, Oklahoma, Cities Service was founded as a public utility, involved in providing natural gas, lighting, and other services. Entering the petroleum business before World War I, Cities Service operated refineries and stations in the East and Midwest. Black and white brand colors changed to green and white in 1946. This is one of Cities Service's earliest signs—note the spelling of "Gasolene."

43

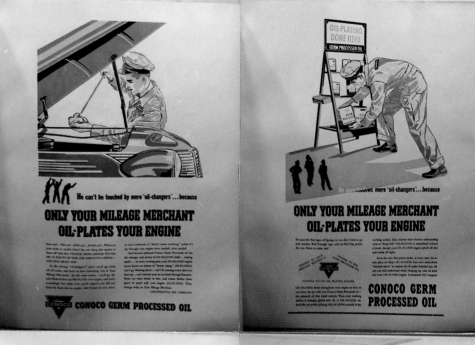

Conoco poster presentation book, circa 1936, hardcover 4" x 5" book with twelve posters demonstrating good work habits, positive attitudes, and products of Conoco "Mileage Merchants," some with three colors, some full color. *Courtesy of Dunbar's Gallery.* Scarce, $300-1,500.

The era when "Service Station" really meant something was the 1930s. Attendants wore uniforms with special hats and bow ties. Tires and oil were checked, air was given free, and windshields were wiped. Many companies, like Conoco, held classes for prospective service men to educate them in the art of service. To differentiate itself, Conoco coined the terms "oil plating" (a concept that sounds far more thorough and complex than oil changing, although it means the same thing) and "Mileage Merchants," meaning service men. This book was used as part of the education of Conoco's service station force. With the advent of self-serve gas stations in the 1950s, the concept of service became lost by the 1970s.

45

Pump Signs

Atlantic Refining Co. porcelain pump sign, diecut fried-egg style with crossed arrows, Philadelphia, Pennsylvania, Red, circa 1925-1932, 9-1/2" x 9-1/2". *Courtesy of Dunbar's Gallery.* $200-800.

Atlantic, originally both a production and refining company, was left with the refining interest as a result of the far-reaching Standard Oil trust busting of 1911. The company started marketing gas in 1915 and spent much time searching for a constant source of crude oil. In the 1930s, Atlantic was responsible for creating some of the most spectacular service stations of all time, using Greek architecture on a grand scale. In 1966, Atlantic, primarily an eastern company, merged with Richfield, a West Coast company, then later with Sinclair. A new trade name emerged, Arco. Later, the Atlantic name was reborn and sold to Sunoco, which uses the Atlantic name in the Northeast today.

Atlantic Premium porcelain pump sign, 1953-1957, 13" x 11". *Courtesy of Dunbar's Gallery.* $50-175.

Atlantic Kerosene porcelain sign, circa 1950s, 13" x 17". *Courtesy of Dunbar's Gallery.* $50-175.

Atlantic porcelain pump sign, circa 1950s, 13" x 9". *Courtesy of Dunbar's Gallery.* $25-100.

46

Chevron Supreme Gasoline porcelain pump sign, 1946-50, 11" x 13". *Courtesy of Dunbar's Gallery.* $100-300.

Part of Standard Oil of California (Socal), the Chevron name was introduced in 1945 in the West.

Cities Service porcelain pump sign, circa 1920s, 10" diameter. *Courtesy of Dunbar's Gallery.* $100-400.

Stamped Veribrite Sign Co., Chicago—one of the largest sign makers of the era.

Cities Service Regular porcelain pump sign, 1950s, 12" x 6". *Courtesy of Dunbar's Gallery.* $25-75.

Conoco die dut porcelain pump sign, circa 1950s, 9-1/2" x 9". *Courtesy of Dunbar's Gallery.* $25-85, *Courtesy of Dunbar's Gallery.*

Cities Service porcelain pump sign, circa 1930s, 9-1/2" diameter, stamped Veribrite Signs. *Courtesy of Dunbar's Gallery.* $100-200.

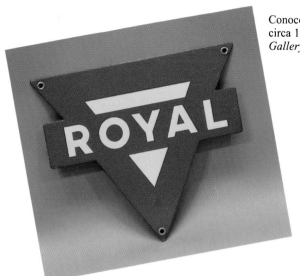

Conoco Royal brand diecut porcelain pump sign, circa 1950s, 10" x 9". *Courtesy of Dunbar's Gallery.* $25-95.

Cargray porcelain pump sign, 10" diameter. *Courtesy of Dunbar's Gallery.* $50-150.

Associated Flying A Gasoline porcelain pump sign, circa 1940s, 10" diameter. *Courtesy of Dunbar's Gallery.* $75-175.

Associated Flying A Super Extra gasoline porcelain pump sign, 10" diameter. *Courtesy of Dunbar's Gallery.* $100-250.
    This one is a bit harder to find than the plain flying a brand.

Associated Flying A Gasoline porcelain pump sign, circa 1950s, 10" x 10". *Courtesy of Dunbar's Gallery.* $100-300.

Associated Flying A porcelain sign, circa 1940s, 14" x 9".
Courtesy of Dunbar's Gallery. $100-350.
This diecut version is also difficult to find.

Tydol Ethyl Flying A Gasoline porcelain pump
sign, circa 1950s, 10" diameter. *Courtesy of
Dunbar's Gallery.* $100-250.

Tydol Flying A Gasoline porcelain pump sign,
unusual mulitcolored style with Flying "A" logo,
circa 1950s, 10" diameter. *Courtesy of Dunbar's
Gallery.* $100-250.

Golden Eagle porcelain pump sign, 13" x 13", circa 1940s.
Courtesy of Dunbar's Gallery. $200-600.
    *A West Coast brand that is highly sought after
by collectors.*

Golden West porcelain pump sign, 10" diameter. *Courtesy of Dunbar's
Gallery.* $150-450.
    *A West Coast company, a group of these signs were found
several years ago and there have been rumblings that this pump
sign has also been reproduced, so beware.*

Gulf Supreme Motor Oil lubester, enamel on steel sign, circa 1920s, 7" diameter. *Courtesy of Dunbar's Gallery.* $200-500.

Before the advent of factory sealed cans, lubesters were storage machines that dispensed motor oil into quart glass bottles that were then placed on racks at the service island. Often, the lubesters had the manufacturing signs on them for instant brand recognition. Today, these signs are extremely collectible, as they are small, usually graphic, and short lived.

That Good Gulf Gasoline porcelain price sign, circa 1920s, 12" diameter. *Courtesy of Dunbar's Gallery.* $300-800.

According to company history, the phrase "that good gulf gasoline" was borne of a letter from a satisfied customer in the early teens inquiring where he could get that "good Gulf gasoline."

Gulf No Nox porcelain pump sign, 10-1/2" x 8-1/2". *Courtesy of Dunbar's Gallery.* $25-50.
In the 1920s, No-Nox was created by Gulf, with anti-knock properties.

That Good Gulf Gasoline porcelain price sign, circa 1920s, 12" diameter. *Courtesy of Dunbar's Gallery.* $300-800.

Gulf chose orange for its tankers because no other company was using that color.

"Good Gulf" porcelain pump sign, 10" diameter, circa 1930s. *Courtesy of Dunbar's Gallery.* $50-125.

Gulf No Nox porcelain pump sign, 10" diameter. *Courtesy of Dunbar's Gallery.* $50-150.

Gulf Dieselect porcelain pump sign, 1950s, 11" x 9". *Courtesy of Dunbar's Gallery.* $25-75.

Gulf New No Nox porcelain pump sign, circa 1950s, 11" x 17". *Courtesy of Dunbar's Gallery.* $50-100.

Husky "Hi Power" single-sided porcelain pump sign, Cody, Wyoming, 12" x 12", circa 1950s. *Courtesy of Dunbar's Gallery.* $200-600.

Husky brand was sold primarily in Wyoming and the Rocky Mountain region.

Husky "Hi Power" single-sided porcelain pump sign, 12" x 12". *Courtesy of Dunbar's Gallery.* $200-600.

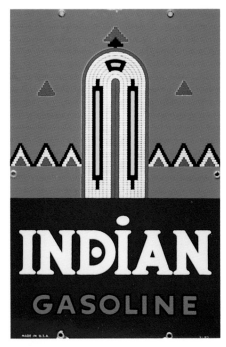

Indian porcelain pump sign, dated 1940, Lawrenceville, Illinois, 12" x 18". *Courtesy of Dunbar's Gallery.* $100-400.
Indian was purchased in the 1930s by Texaco for its Havoline brand products. Texaco made Indian until 1942, as a cheaper brand of gasoline. But the sign is great!

Iso-Vis Motor Oil lubester porcelain sign, circa 1930s, Standard Oil Co., Indiana, 7" diameter, double sided. *Courtesy of Dunbar's Gallery.* Scarce, $200-450.

Jenney Solvenized porcelain pump sign, circa 1930s, 11" diameter. *Courtesy of Dunbar's Gallery.* $300-900.
One of Jenney's two most graphic pump signs, the other being for their aviation gas.

Midway Superior porcelain pump sign, 11" x 11".
Courtesy of Dunbar's Gallery. $100-300.

Mobilgas porcelain pump sign, dated 1947, 11" x 12".
Courtesy of Dunbar's Gallery. $50-200.
   A pump sign that is being reproduced.

Mobiloil "E" Gargoyle lubester porcelain pump
sign,1920s, 9" diameter. *Courtesy of Dunbar's Gallery.*
$100-500.
   *I don't know what the difference is between
Fords and other makes, which makes this
demarcation necessary. My guess is marketing
and the association of being used in America's
favorite cars.*

Mobilfuel diesel porcelain pump sign, dated 1954, 11" x
11". *Courtesy of Dunbar's Gallery.* $100-300.

Mother Penn lubester porcelain flange sign, Dryer Clark and Dryer, Oklahoma City, Oklahoma, circa 1930s, 8-1/2" x 6". *Courtesy of Dunbar's Gallery.* $300-800.
This is the smaller of two sizes made for this lubester sign.

Pacer 200 Hi-Test porcelain pump sign, 8" x 12", South Bend, Indiana, 1950s. *Courtesy of Dunbar's Gallery.* $100-175.

Pan Am service station porcelain pump sign, circa 1940s, 13" x 13", part of Amoco. *Courtesy of Dunbar's Gallery.* $75-150.

Pure Premium and Pure Pep porcelain pump signs, both 1940s-50s, 10" x 12". *Courtesy of Dunbar's Gallery.* Each $50-75.

Rocolene lubester oil rack enamel on steel
sign, circa 1930s, 7" diameter. *Courtesy of
Dunbar's Gallery.* $100-300.

Republic Royale regular porcelain pump sign,
circa 1940s, 10" x 11". *Courtesy of Dunbar's
Gallery.* $75-150.

Shamrock Trailmaster regular porcelain pump sign,
circa 1950s, 10-1/2" x 12-1/2". *Courtesy of Dunbar's
Gallery.* $50-150.

Shamrock Cloud Master regular porcelain pump sign,
circa 1950s, 10-1/2" x 12-1/2". *Courtesy of Dunbar's
Gallery.* $50-150.

Sterling Ethyl Gasoline porcelain pump sign, circa 1940s, St. Mary's, West Virginia, 12" x 10". *Courtesy of Dunbar's Gallery.* $100-200.

Sterling merged with Quaker State in 1931 and continued to market gas under the Sterling brand name.

Sinclair Gasoline porcelain pump sign, circa 1950s, 12" x 14". *Courtesy of Dunbar's Gallery.* $25-100.

Sunoco Motor Oil "Mercury Made" porcelain sign, circa 1920s-30s, 10" x 12". *Courtesy of Dunbar's Gallery.* $100-350.

Sun Oil Co. hails from Philadelphia, Pennsylvania. They began their marketing operation in 1920, expanding from the Northeast to the Midwest and South in the 1930s.

Swifty Genuine Ethyl porcelain pump sign, circa 1950s, 9" x 11". *Courtesy of Dunbar's Gallery.* $50-150.

Sunoco Dynafuel porcelain diamond pump sign, circa 1940s, 12" x 7". *Courtesy of Dunbar's Gallery.* $50-150.
A whole bunch of these were found in 1997 and it will take time for them to be assimilated into collections. Until then, it's a very inexpensive sign to buy.

Blue Sunoco porcelain pump sign, diamond shaped, circa 1940s, 12" x 8". *Courtesy of Dunbar's Gallery.* $75-175.

    This is a more difficult Sunoco pump sign to find than the Dynafuel.

Sunoco 200 porcelain diecut pump sign, 1950s, 15" x 20". *Courtesy of Dunbar's Gallery.* $100-300.

    For a number of years, the company only sold Blue Sunoco, a high grade gasoline.

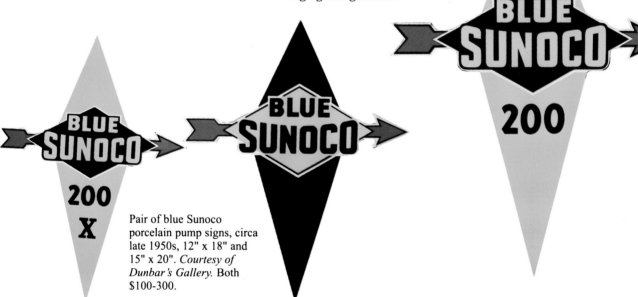

Pair of blue Sunoco porcelain pump signs, circa late 1950s, 12" x 18" and 15" x 20". *Courtesy of Dunbar's Gallery.* Both $100-300.

Texaco lubester porcelain sign, circa 1920s, double sided, 5" diameter. *Courtesy of Dunbar's Gallery.* $200-600.

Texaco porcelain pump sign, dated 1930, 8" diameter. *Courtesy of Dunbar's Gallery.* $100-300.

Texaco Fire Chief porcelain pump sign, dated 1957, 10" x 15". *Courtesy of Dunbar's Gallery.* $25-100. *This is a pretty easy sign to find for the new collector.*

Texaco Sky Chief Supreme porcelain pump sign, dated 1959, 12" x 18". *Courtesy of Dunbar's Gallery.* $75-150.

Texaco Diesel Chief tin pump sign, circa 1960s, 15" x 9". *Courtesy of Dunbar's Gallery.* $75-150.

Texaco Sea Chief tin pump sign, circa 1960s, 15" x 9". *Courtesy of Dunbar's Gallery.* $75-150.

Time Premium porcelain pump sign, circa
1940s, 9-1/2" x 14". *Courtesy of Dunbar's
Gallery.* $150-350.
    *Signs from this California company
are very desirable.*

Union 76 Gasoline porcelain pump sign, circa 1940s,
11" diameter. *Courtesy of Dunbar's Gallery.* $50-100.
    *Union, a West Coast company that began at
the turn of the century, merged with Pure Oil Co.
in 1965 and the corporate name became Unocal
in 1983.*

Pair Wolf's Head Oil enamel on steel lubester signs,
Heavy and Medium, 1930s, Oil City, Pennsylvania, 8".
Courtesy of Dunbar's Gallery. $150-450 each.
    *First an oil producer, Wolverine marketed
gasoline under the Empire name in the late 1920s.
Pennzoil purchased the company in 1963 and kept
the Wolf's Head name and logo.*

Service Signs and Posters

1912 Columbia Ignitor Dry Cells poster and calendar, 18" x 32" *Courtesy of Dunbar's Gallery.* Rare, $2,000-5,000.

By the looks of this poster, one may think the devil was the inventor of the battery. Instead, it was an Italian physicist, Alessandro Volta, who, in the last 1700s, created a device that could transfer charges to other objects. In honor of his invention, the unit of electric potential, the volt, was named after him.

Columbia Batteries tin flange sign, patented 1910, 18-1/4" x 13". *Courtesy of Dunbar's Gallery.* Scarce, $300-1,000.

Robert Bosch (1861-1942), a German industrialist, manufactured the first ignition system, introducing the high voltage magneto in 1903. Meanwhile, in the states, Charles Kettering, developed the self starter using a battery and induction coil, eliminating the handcrank and saving countless drivers fractured wrists and broken jaws.

Optician porcelain sign, featuring The Autoglas, patented 1911, 30" x 9" *Courtesy of Dunbar's Gallery.* Rare, $600-1,500.

With the advent of the automobile came the advent of automobilie accessories. As the first vehicles had no windshields, goggles or glass were imperative to keep out dust, flies, rain, oil spatters, and the occasional angry farmer's fist.

Pair of Bosch signs: Official Bosch Sales and Service porcelain sign, circa 1920, 16" x 12". $200-700. Bosch Sales and Service porcelain sign, circa 1920, 15" x 24". $200-700. *Bob & Judy Palmerino Collection, Courtesy of Noel Barrett Auctions.*

Bosch is a huge name in magnetos. The Europeans used his ignition system, while American manufacturers used Kettering's invention. Bosch also helped to develop spark plugs, windshield-wiper motors, and fuel injection systems for all types of transportation.

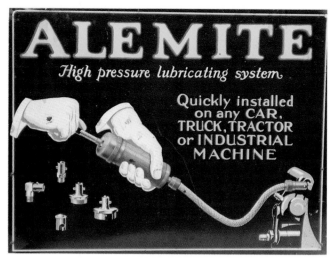

Alemite lubricant system tin sign, circa 1920s, 16" x 12".
Courtesy of Dunbar's Gallery. $200-700.

Alemite, of Chicago, got started in the early teens and was in business until the early 1970s.

We Install the Boyce Motometer 'Free,' litho tin on cardboard sign, circa 1910, 19" x 27". *Bob & Judy Palmerino Collection, Courtesy of Noel Barrett Auctions.* $500-2,500.

Motometers were the forerunners of dash instruments, measuring the temperature of the engine to prevent overheating. Motometers themselves are extremely collectible.

Stop Here for Raybestos Brakes flange tin sign, circa 1920s, 18" x 14". *Courtesy of Dunbar's Gallery.* $100-50.

Until 1930, brakes were applied mechanically. With the advent of hydraulic brakes, in which hydraulic fluid in the master cylinder is pushed through the brake lines to the wheels in proportion to pressure applied on the brake pedal, braking became much smoother and more even.

Effecto Auto Finishes, Pratt & Lambert, tin and iron sign, circa 1915, 25" diameter. *Courtesy of Dunbar's Gallery.* $100-300.

Unlike Henry Ford, who manufactured millions of Model Ts in black, the rest of the automobile world loved color on their cars.

Acme Quality Motor Car Finish metal sign, litho on tin, circa 1920, 20" x 7". *Bob & Judy Palmerino Collection, Courtesy of Noel Barrett Auctions.* $500-1,000.

Although this is a Model T, I'm sure the Acme White Lead Co. offered an array of colors.

Clossman Hardware Co. embossed litho tin sign, circa mid-1920s, 29-1/2" x 21-1/2", framed. *Courtesy of Dunbar's Gallery.* $300-700.

Steelcote Rubber Enamel Car Bumper display, circa late 1930s, cardboard easel sign with metal attachments, 20" x 30". *Bob & Judy Palmerino Collection, Courtesy of Noel Barrett Auctions. V*ery unusual display and rare in this condition, $400-800.

Automobiles have been marketed alternately as necessary transportation, vehicles of escape from a narrow life, and an extension of one's own personality. Choice of colors here help to redefine one's own predilections, unless, of course, you're boring and choose black.

Solder Seal Radiator Service porcelain sign, circa 1920, 18" x 12". *Courtesy of Dunbar's Gallery.* Rare and early, $200-600.

Why do cars need radiators? Simple—engines produce far more heat than the engine can convert into useful power. To prevent the engine from overheating, a coolant called antifreeze must be circulated with water by a radiator. Radiator tynes can part or become worn from constant use, heat, etc., and that's where leak repair comes in.

Wonder Worker Motor Car Necessities display sign, 36" x 10-1/2". *Courtesy of Dunbar's Gallery.* $100-250.
This was originally a rack display sign.

Edison Mazda automobile lamp counter display, litho tin on wooden base, 14" x 24". B*ob & Judy Palmerino Collection, Courtesy of Noel Barrett Auctions.* $200-600.

Gilmer Fan Belt counter display, circa 1920s, litho on tin, with image of "Happy Van, the Gilmer Man." 16" x 26" x 22". B*ob & Judy Palmerino Collection, Courtesy of Noel Barrett Auctions.* $200-600.

Perfect Circle Oil Hog tin sign, by artist Tony Sarg, 29" x 36" circa 1930s. B*ob & Judy Palmerino Collection, Courtesy of Noel Barrett Auctions.* $500-1,500.
Tony Sarg was a great American artist who also created marionettes. It's exceedingly rare to find an automotive sign with such detail, and rarer to find one signed and by a well known artist.

Stromberg Carburetors Sales & Service porcelain sign, double sided, circa 1930s, 36" diameter. B*ob & Judy Palmerino Collection, Courtesy of Noel Barrett Auctions.* $400-1,000.
Vincent Bendix, another great American inventor, developed a drive mechanism that helped make the Kettering's self-starter possible. In 1912, he founded the Bendix Brake Co. Besides brakes, Bendix is known for advances in aviation electronics and air race sponsorship.

Prestone Anti Freeze porcelain thermometer, 1930s, 10" diameter. *Courtesy of Dunbar's Gallery.* Mint, scarce, $100-400.

Wilhelm Maybach, a German engineer for Daimler cars and Zeppelin engines, also developed the honeycomb radiator in 1900. Prestone antifreeze is still produced and marketed worldwide today.

Weed chains "Gas Today" tin sign, circa 1920s, 16" x 24". *Courtesy of Dunbar's Gallery.* $200-600.

As less than 10 percent of the nation's highways were paved by 1920, a device was needed to help autos navigate mud, snow, and ice. Chains give tires more traction to grip slippery surfaces and are still used today on certain all-terrain vehicles in extreme conditions.

Weed Chains standup cardboard litho store display, circa 1920s, electrified, 21" x 30". *Courtesy of Dunbar's Gallery.* $200-400.

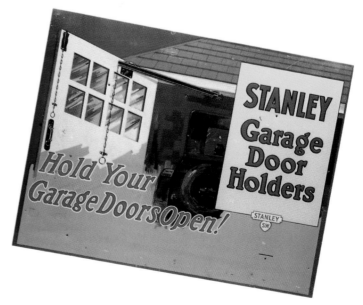

Stanley Garage Door Holders tin sign, 35" x 27", circa late 1920s. *Courtesy of Dunbar's Gallery.* $200-500.
Forerunner to the battery powered garage door opener.

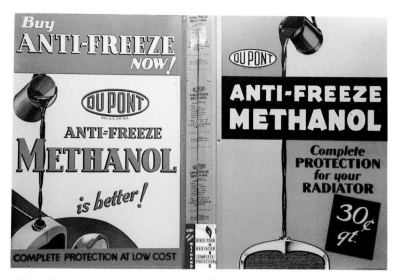

Pair of Dupont Methanol posters, circa 1920s, unused in original mailer with booklets, banners, and chart, 20" x 28". *Courtesy of Dunbar's Gallery.* $100-200 pair.

The Dupont Co. got its start in 1802 producing gunpowder. Pierre Dupont added paints, cellophane, and nylon to its list of products. He was GM president from 1920-23, and owned a sizable chunk of GM stock until forced to divest in 1961. This close partnership is why Dupont paints are used on GM cars.

General Dual Balloon tire poster, 25" x 38". *Courtesy of Dunbar's Gallery.* Rare, $300-1,000.

Oldfield Tires porcelain flange sign, 21" x 16". *Bob & Judy Palmerino Collection, Courtesy of Noel Barrett Auctions.* Rare, $500-2,000.

Berna "Barney" Oldfield was a race car driver who spread the racing craze in the United States. He raced bicycles professionally in the late 1800s. In 1902 he joined the Ford factory racing team and in 1903 became the first person to reach the speed of 60 mph. Later, Oldfield was the first person to drive a 100-mph lap at the Indianapolis Speedway; and at Daytona Beach, Fla., on Mar. 16, 1910, he established a world land speed record for the measured mile at 131.724 mph. Oldfield retired from racing in 1918 and started an automobile tire manufacturing business which was never quite as successful as his racing career.

Morgan Wright Tires litho poster, copyright 1916, "Want to take a ride on good tires?", 23" x 27", framed. *Bob & Judy Palmerino Collection, Courtesy of Noel Barrett Auctions.* $200-800.

Great image of beckoning boy in duster and goggles, which sums up the excitement of motoring, especially in the early days.

"Keep Smiling with Kellys" tin tire holder and sign, Miss "Lotta Miles", 16" x 9" *Courtesy of Dunbar's Gallery.* $200-500.

Kelly's heyday was the 1920s. Lotta Miles was the best tire logo by far, with a beautiful face, a classic cloche hat, and a slightly risqué open blouse. Signs with this logo are highly sought after by collectors.

Kelly-Springfield Tractor Tires oval tin sign, 35" x 22". *Courtesy of Dunbar's Gallery.* $50-150.

In contrast to Lotta Miles, this sign is a lotta boring. Signs without graphics are always worth a lot less and are a lot less desirable, as they have much less visual appeal.

Fisk Tire double sided wooden sign, circa 1920, black wood frame, 30" x 42". *Courtesy of Dunbar's Gallery.* Rare, exceptional, $200-600.

Although WC Fields couldn't stand them, children make for great logos and salesmen. The image of sleepy boy and security tire make a great statement. Michelin is making that same statement today in their commercials.

Fisk Tire litho on carboard sign, circa 1920s, 18" x 22". Framed, *Bob & Judy Palmerino Collection, Courtesy of Noel Barrett Auctions.* $200-600.

Fisk Tire sign, circa 1930s, 38" x 32". *Courtesy of Dunbar's Gallery.* $100-350.

Fisk Tire store window display, litho on cardboard, with separate standup pieces, circa 1930s, 62" x 35". *Courtesy of Dunbar's Gallery.* $150-450.

For a new consumer society in the throes of the Depression, any kind of a purchase was a major event. Any good sales department was part performer, part prevaricator, part cheerleader.

Michelin Tires & Tubes porcelain sign, circa 1930s, 60" x 18". *Courtesy of Dunbar's Gallery.* $500-1,500.

Andre and Edouard Michelin manufactured France's first pneumatic tires. They offered experimental tires to a bicycle racer in 1891. The bicyclist won, and by 1892 the company boasted 10,000 new customers. In 1895, the brothers put their tires on a Daimler automobile that they drove in the Paris-Bordeaux auto race. In 1905, the company introduced tire tread patterns; demountable wheel rims in 1906; low-pressure "balloon" tires in 1923; steel-cord tires in 1938, and, steel-belted radial tires in 1949. Michelin remains an innovator.

Michelin Tires tin sign, circa 1920s, framed, probably Canadian, 36" x 12". *Courtesy of Dunbar's Gallery.* $300-700.

We know him as the Michelin Man, but his real name is Bibendum or Mr. Bib, first introduced in 1896. On his first poster, Mr. Bib held a champagne glass and toasted "Now we drink.to your health. Instead of a nice vintage Dom Perignon, the glass held broken glass and nails. The point was that Mr. Bib could pick up anything on the road and keep on rolling. Michelin uses his image to this day. If you're in France and have a bit of a paunchy stomach, that's called a Michelin, and I would suggest avoiding swallowing sharp objects.

Michelin Tires enamel on steel shield sign, circa 1940s, 24" x 32". *Courtesy of Dunbar's Gallery.* $200-500.

The first pneumatic tire was patented in 1845 by Robert Thomson. For those of you wanting and needing a history of the tire, John Dunlop, a Scottish veteriarian, patented a pneumatic tire for bicycles in 1888 and founded a company to manufacture tires for bicycles and automobiles. By 1900 and the dawn of the automobile age, tires had round cross-sections, separate inner tubes inflated to a pressure of 70 pounds per square inch, and rubber-coated and cotton-cloth covers. Treads, patterns which lessened the danger of sideslip, were introduced 10 years later in 1910. Layers of reinforcing cord date from the 1920s; whitewalls followed in 1929. "Balloon" tires ran at a lower inflation pressure and gave a smoother ride than their earlier counterparts. The 1930s saw the introduction of synthetic materials in tire construction. The last major change—elimination of separate inner tubes—came in 1954.

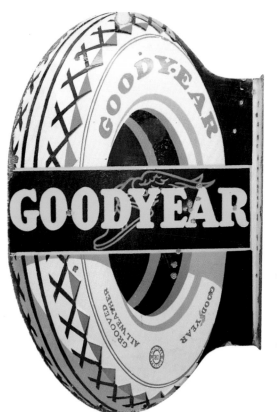

Goodyear Tires porcelain flange sign, circa 1920s, 23" x 33". *Courtesy of Dunbar's Gallery.* Rare, $400-1,500.

Like many of his manufacturing brethren, Charles Goodyear never was a part of the tire empire that exists to this day. Goodyear was an inventor and spent time in debtor's prison. He developed a process to cure Indian rubber so that it would be durable and not decompose or melt. He patented the vulcanization process in 1839.

Goodyear Tires litho tin flange sign, circa 1920s, winged foot logo, 22" x 12". *Courtesy of Dunbar's Gallery.* $100-450.

Charles Goodyear died in 1860, 38 years before Frank Sieberling bought an old power plant in Akron, Ohio, and began producing tires with his brother. Like others had done, he named the company after the inventor of vulcanization. By 1908, with the explosion of the auto industry, Goodyear was doing more than $2 million in annual sales.

Goodyear Tires tin sign, circa 1920s, 27-1/2" x 10". *Courtesy of Dunbar's Gallery.* $100-300.

We may think the official Goodyear symbol is the blimp, but Frank Sieberling chose Mercury's winged foot as Goodyear's logo in 1900, and it is used to this day. Goodyear began making airplane tires in 1909 and fabricated the rubberized material for early dirigibles, such as the Akron, which, in 1912, exploded after only a few minutes of flight.

Goodyear Tires cardboard stand up display, circa 1930, 20" x 30". *Courtesy of Dunbar's Gallery.* $200-500.

Many companies changed their advertising campaigns during the Depression. In the 1920s, approaches were more lighthearted. In the 1930s they reflecting the frantic mood of the country, focusing on the apocalyptic, i.e., buy this or your life will be destroyed. As most could only afford necessities, now every product was portrayed as a necessity.

Goodyear Service Station porcelain sign, 72" x 24", framed. *Courtesy of Dunbar's Gallery.* Scarce, $400-1,800.

The balloon hugging the globe is meant to symbolize that the world rides on Goodyear Tires, still one of the world's largest tire companies.

Goodyear Service Station porcelain diecut flange sign, circa 1920s, 26" x 28". *Courtesy of Dunbar's Gallery.* $400-1,500.

Frank Sieberling was riding high until 1921, until a post war recession sliced sales in half. At 62, the president was forced out. Instead of retiring, Sieberling went out and raised the funds to start his own business, the Sieberling Tire and Rubber Co., in Ohio and Pennsylvania. Within ten years, it was grossing more than $42 million in worldwide sales. Sieberling ran his company until 1950, when he retired at age 90. In 1964, nine years after Sieberling died, Goodyear bought the Sieberling Rubber Co.

Goodyear Tire porcelain sign, circa 1930, single sided, framed, 46" x 40". *Courtesy of Dunbar's Gallery.* $400-1,200.

More People Ride on Goodyear Tires porcelain sign, circa 1930s, 22" diameter. *Courtesy of Dunbar's Gallery.* $100-400.

This is a claim the company can still make today.

Goodyear Tires Tubes Accessories Selected Dealer porcelain sign, made in Canada, 36" x 60". *Courtesy of Dunbar's Gallery.* Scarce, $400-1,800.

Goodyear has had a worldwide presence since the early 1900s. At one time Canadian and Eurpoean signs weren't as collectible or valuable as American ones, but that is changing quickly.

70

Goodyear Tires porcelain display rack sign, circa 1930s, 14" x 9".
Courtesy of Dunbar's Gallery. $100-350.

Goodrich Safety Tires "Canadian Mountie" porcelain sign, circa 1920s, 20" x 55". *Courtesy of Dunbar's Gallery.* Rare, $2,000-6,000.

Goodrich was the first rubber company founded in Akron, Ohio, which is now home to several hundred plastics, chemical, and rubber companies. Benjamin Goodrich was an army surgeon in the Civil War. He bought the plant n 1870 and began producing rubber goods.

Goodrich Tires porcelain sign, circa 1920s, 19" x 27". *Courtesy of Dunbar's Gallery.* $300-1,300.

Goodrich entered the tire market about the same time as Goodyear. Like its counterpart, Goodrich ventured into many markets, including zippers. Originally known as the hookless fastener, Goodrich bought the company that made them, put them on galoshes and then on Navy flight suits, beginning the first zipper craze.

Goodrich Tires Silvertowns porcelain flange sign, 1930s, 23" x 19". *Courtesy of Dunbar's Gallery.* $100-400.

Like most companies, Goodrich gave a hook to its tires, calling them Silvertowns.

Goodrich Tires porcelain sign, 1930s, 48" x 12". *Courtesy of Dunbar's Gallery.* $100-300.

Goodrich and Goodyear are known best for tires, but they are rubber companies first. Goodrich helped changed the way golf was played when the company developed a lighter, tightly rubber threaded ball that could be hit farther than the gutta-percha style that had been used in the 19th Century.

Firestone Tires porcelain sign, late 1930s type tire, framed, 30" x 40". *Courtesy of Dunbar's Gallery.* Scarce, $400-1,500.

Seated on the Cuyahoga River, Akron has become the tire capital of the world. In 1900, Harvey Firestone founded his company in the town of Goodyear and Goodrich. He was president of Firestone until 1932. Firestone first became interested in rubber while selling buggies for his uncle. Firestone combatted the other big names by becoming the major supplier for Ford cars in 1906, thus ensuring the company's viability.

Firestone Balloon Tire Christmas cardboard display, circa 1930s, 18" x 34". *Courtesy of Dunbar's Gallery.* $100-300.

Firestone first introduced detachable rims and balloon tires in 1923.

Firestone Gum Dipped Tires porcelain sign, 48" x 20", circa 1920. *Courtesy of Dunbar's Gallery.* Scarce, $300-1,000.

Advertising slogans either focused on safety or value. By the early 1930s, Firestone was supplying a quarter of the tires used in the United States.

Firestone Ground Grip Farm Tires porcelain flange sign, circa 1930s, 24" x 18". *Bob & Judy Palmerino Collection, Courtesy of Noel Barrett Auctions.* Scarce, $500-1,500.

Firestone porcelain sign, made for the Winchester Auto Co. of Massachusetts, 36" x 30". *Courtesy of Dunbar's Gallery.* $200-600.
    Here Firestone goes for value with a slogan that must have pleased compatriot Henry Ford.

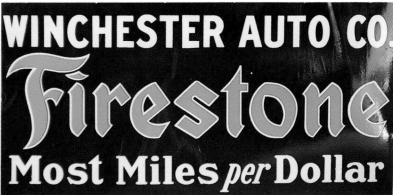

Firestone Tires diecut porcelain shield, double sided, 36" x 30". *Courtesy of Dunbar's Gallery.* $100-400.

Gillette Tires embossed tin sign, circa 1930s, 19" x 72". *Courtesy of Dunbar's Gallery.* $200-500.
    Like every new industry, a number of companies jumped on board, only to see a huge shakeout when market demand couldn't meet the overwhelming supply.

Diamond Tires tin flange sign, 1920s, 18" x 27". *Courtesy of Dunbar's Gallery.* Scarce, $200-800.
    Many companies tried to come up with their own distinctive names and phrases to differentiate them from all the others, hence, the rise of the logo. Here, we see "Squeegee" which is used for windshield service nowadays.

Miller Tires display, circa 1930s, 52" x 36". *Courtesy of Dunbar's Gallery.* $200-500.

Cooper Tires tin upright sign, circa 1950s-60s, 12" x 60". *Courtesy of Dunbar's Gallery.* $50-100.

Cooper Tires enamel on steel sign, circa 1950s-60s, 36" x 18". *Courtesy of Dunbar's Gallery.* $50-150.
You can see this logo today, with the shield of armor.

Cities Service/Acme Tires enamel on steel sign, dated 1937, 17" x 59". *Courtesy of Dunbar's Gallery.* $100-400.

With the rise of uniform service stations, many gas and oil companies realized that they could further their profits by offering other services and related products, such as tires.

Wards Riverside Tires tin thermometer with owl, 13". *Courtesy of Dunbar's Gallery.* $30-100.

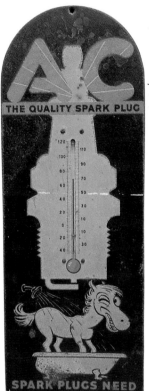

AC Spark Plug enamel on steel thermometer, circa 1930s, 6" x 16". *Courtesy of Dunbar's Gallery.* $100-300.

Sparkplug is also known as comic strip figure Barney Google's sidekick. AC licensed Sparkplug to sell their wares, a good choice. In signs, this logo is highly desirable.

AC Spark Plug enamel on steel flange sign, circa 1940s. *Courtesy of Dunbar's Gallery.* $100-400.

AC Flexible Lines garage display, circa 1950s, 16" x 9". *Courtesy of Dunbar's Gallery.* $50-100.

AC Spark Plugs tin sign, 1940s, 8" x 18". *Courtesy of Dunbar's Gallery.* $50-200.

AC Fuel Pumps enamel on steel flange sign, 1960s, 15" x 11". *Courtesy of Dunbar's Gallery.* $25-100.

Prest-o-lite Sales and Service enamel on steel flange sign, 18" x 26". *Courtesy of Dunbar's Gallery.* $100-400.

Prest-o-lite Sales and Service porcelain doorpush, 4" x 11-1/2". *Courtesy of Dunbar's Gallery. Rare size, $100-400.*
It's very rare to find service station doorpushes, which makes this, along with the great graphics, a sought after sign.

Champion Spark Plug porcelain sign, 28" x 34", circa 1940. *Courtesy of Dunbar's Gallery. Rare, $200-800.*
This is a great service station sign because it's colorful and dynamic, plus it has a thermometer and weather forecast and service check wheels.

Champion Spark Plug enamel on steel sign, 29" x 14". *Courtesy of Dunbar's Gallery.* $100-400.

A few of these were found in mint condition, but have long since been assimilated into collections.

Champion Spark Plug enamel on steel sign, 10" x 27". *Courtesy of Dunbar's Gallery.* $100-400.

One way to tell earlier from later signs is the amount of detailing. Later signs will generally be simpler.

Perrine Batteries embossed tin sign, 19" x 13-1/2", framed. *Courtesy of Dunbar's Gallery.* $100-300.

The polar bear was a popular logo, hardy in all types of weather.

Delco Battery figural enamel on steel sign, 23" x 16-1/2". *Courtesy of Dunbar's Gallery.* $50-150.

Charles Kettering is one of the many unsung heroes of the early 20th Century. In 1905, while working at the National Cash Register Co., he designed the first electric cash register. In 1908 he developed an improved ignition system. In 1911, Kettering founded Delco, Dayton Engineering Laboratories Co. Soon after, he produced the first practical electric self-starter for Cadillac. In 1919, Kettering became the director of research at General Motors and guided many important research projects, including high-octane gasoline and the lightweight two-cycle diesel engine. Delco has remained an important part of the GM family, manufacturing a number of the electrical and mechanical systems for GM to this day. Along with GM president Alfred Sloan, Kettering was co-founder of the Sloan Kettering Hospital for cancer research, another enduring legacy.

Trico Windshield Wipers enamel on steel flange sign, 23" x 15". *Courtesy of Dunbar's Gallery. $50-150.*

With the advent of the electric motor, windshield wipers were developed by Robert Bosch and others in the early 1900s.

Exide Battery tin sign, 57" x 34". *Courtesy of Dunbar's Gallery. $50-150.*

This is a good example of a very basic sign with no graphics or excitement, therefore not nearly as collectible as a sign that features a logo.

Sealed Power Piston Rings tin thermometer, 6" x 26". *Courtesy of Dunbar's Gallery. $50-150.*

There are some collectors who simply look for thermometers. These lasted longer at stations, because they provided a function as well as advertising.

Simonize store card, 1940s green Oldsmobile convertible, two young women watch an older man wax his car, 10-1/2" x 12-1/2"; Simonize store card, 1940s maroon Pontiac sedan, young woman helps older man wax car, 8" x 10". *Courtesy of Dunbar's Gallery. $10-40 each.*

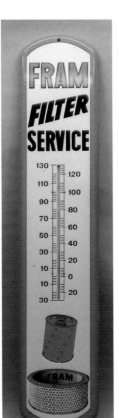

Fram Filter Service tin thermometer, 8" x 39".
Courtesy of Dunbar's Gallery. $50-150.

Dependable Champion Sparkplug Service enamel on steel flange sign, 18" x
12". *Courtesy of Dunbar's Gallery.* $50-150.

Goodyear Tires belt rack, circa
1970s, 24" x 18". *Courtesy of
Dunbar's Gallery.* $20-75.

Pair of Michelin tire racks, circa 1970s, 12" x 7". *Courtesy of Dunbar's Gallery.* $25-100.

Goodyear tin sign, circa 1970s, 32" x 12".
Courtesy of Dunbar's Gallery. $25-50.

Dunlop Tires tin sign, circa
1970s, 58" x 14". *Courtesy
of Dunbar's Gallery.* $25-75.

Bridgestone tire rack, circa 1970s,
15" x 10" x 9" diameter. *Courtesy of
Dunbar's Gallery.* $25-75.

Cities Service tin tire display holder, circa 1950s, 8" x 21". *Courtesy of Dunbar's Gallery.*
$25-100.

Chapter 2

Oil Cans, Station Displays

On August 27, 1859, the first barrel of bubbling crude petroleum was drilled in Titusville, Pennsylvania. Almost 130 years later, its byproduct of gas and oil compose the lifeblood of our transporation system. After all, who wants to go back to pedal power?

Once other sites were discovered and drilling companies formed, the next problem was refining the products, to be followed by marketing and distillation. With the infant automobile market, companies had to guess the amounts of gas and oil that the motorists would use and how many would use them at all.

When the automotive market took off in the early- to mid-teens, with Henry Ford's cheap Tin Lizzie, so did gas stations. They appeared on the curbsides of every town, run by the general store or an independent operator. Gas was drawn from very crudely made visible gas pumps, which measured the gas more or less (usually less if the owner was dishonest) correctly. Lubesters machines dispensed oil in large refillable glass jars.

By 1939, the gas and oil industry was getting its act under control. Official service stations built by national companies such as Texaco, Gulf, and Mobil assured the customers that they were being treated fairly. The standard size for oil cans was deemed to be one quart—these cans replaced the earlier glass bottles. To combat dropping sales due to the Depression, these companies offered more services and repairs to compensate for lost profits.

Amazingly many of the major companies of the era still thrive today and are very collectible for their long history. These include Shell, Sunoco, Gulf, Texaco, Mobil, and Phillips 66. Other companies are collected for the opposite reason—they didn't last, or at least not long in one configuration, so the advertising and containers of their products are rare.

As you can imagine, the early bottles are sought after, but still offer good value, as the bottles range from $5-150 each. Full racks, however, with porcelain signs, fetch a lot more money. Early oil cans tend to bring more money than bottles. I don't know if that's due to their colorful lithography or whether bottles just haven't had their day yet. One-quart oil cans can be bought for as little as $10 and as much as $1,000, depending, as always, on rarity and condition.

Endurance Motor Oil two-gallon tin, circa 1920s, four sided. *Courtesy of Dunbar's Gallery.* $100-350.

Texaco Motor Oil under-the-seat tin, circa 1920s, 7-1/2" x 5-1/2" x 2-1/2". *Courtesy of Dunbar's Gallery.* $100-350.

Underseat tins were the first ones used and designed this way because, well, they fit nicely under the seat. By the way, here's an easy way to tell the approximate age of a Texaco sign: If the center "T" in the star logo is outlined in black, it's pre-1939. If it's outlined in white, it's later. Many are stamped with a date.

Gulf Supreme Heavy Motor Oil underseat tin, 1920s, 8-1/2" x 5-1/2" x 5". *Courtesy of Dunbar's Gallery.* $200-400.

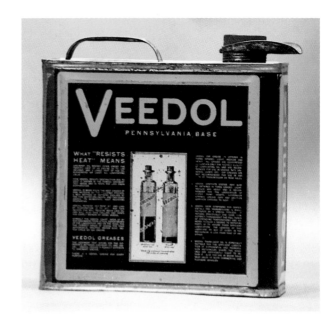

Veedol one gallon oil can, 1920s, with cap, 9-1/2" x 10" x 3". *Courtesy of Dunbar's Gallery.* $50-150.
This can has shown up in quantity, but the condition greatly varies.

Oilzum half-gallon under-the-seat service can, circa 1915-20, tin with soldered seams, Oilzum Man logo on both ends and both sides, original pour spout and screw in plug, 13" x 3" square. *Courtesy of Dunbar's Gallery.* Scarce, $300-900.
This is a very early under-the-seat tin, as can be seen by the Cylinder Oil can shown on the other side of Waldo.

Oilzum Gas Engine Cylinder five-gallon oil can, circa 1920, with Oilzum Man logo on two sides, 9" x 14" x 9". *Courtesy of Dunbar's Gallery.* $200-400.
Another scarce and early Oilzum tin.

Streamline Motor Oil two-gallon oil can, with 1930s coupe, 11" x 8-1/2" x 5". *Courtesy of Dunbar's Gallery.* $200-500.

EN-AR-CO Refinery Sealed Motor Oil five-quart can, circa 1940s. *Courtesy of Dunbar's Gallery.* $450-150.

Pep Boys Motor Oil two-gallon oil can, 1930s, 11" x 8-1/2" x 5". *Courtesy of Dunbar's Gallery.* $150-350.

Manny, Moe, and Jack, the automotive accessories world's answer to the Three Stooges. Based on the West Coast, the Pep Boys built a great string of franchises, capped off by their Pep Boys products, packaged in bright colors.

Mobiloil Artic Special tin, in English and Japanese, circa 1920s. *Courtesy of Dunbar's Gallery.* Scarce, $150-350.

Lindbergh used Mobiloil in his flight across the Atlantic.

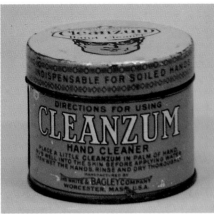

Cleanzum tin, Oilzum Man face on cover and side, 2-1/2" x 3" diameter. *Courtesy of Dunbar's Gallery.* $50-125.
What should you should after you Oilzum? Cleanzum, man, cleanzum.

Oilzum Motor Oil five-quart can, circa 1930s, 10" tall. *Courtesy of Dunbar's Gallery.* $100-300.

Oilzum Motor Oil five-quart can, circa 1930s, round with earlier Oilzum Man logo, 10". *Courtesy of Dunbar's Gallery.* $200-400.

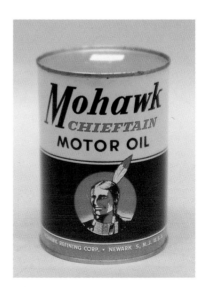

Mohawk Chieftain Motor Oil one-quart can. *Courtesy of Dunbar's Gallery.* $25-75.
One-quart cans were developed and produced in the 1930s, rendering glass bottles obsolete.

Oilzum Water Pump one-pound lubricant can, 5" tall. *Courtesy of Dunbar's Gallery.* $50-125.

Nourse Motor Oil one-quart can, Kansas City, Missouri. *Courtesy of Dunbar's Gallery.* $25-75.

There have been hundreds of independent oil and gas companies. As in other industries, many have merged or been bought by larger corporations.

Bison Motor Oil one-quart can. *Courtesy of Dunbar's Gallery.* $25-75.

Capitol chain and cup grease one-pound tin, 3-1/2" diameter x 4-1/2". *Courtesy of Dunbar's Gallery.* $25-75.

Lehi Lube motor oil two-gallon tin. *Courtesy of Dunbar's Gallery.* $25-75.

Mobiloil Authorized Service Gargoyle oil rack, circa 1920s, 25" x 30" x 20" diameter. *Courtesy of Dunbar's Gallery.* Rare, $500-2,000.

Mobiloil "Arctic" eight "Filpruf" bottle rack, 1920s, has eight complete Arctic Diamond Quart Bottles with "Filpruf" pourers and caps, Gargoyle logo. *Courtesy of Dunbar's Gallery.* $500-1,000.

Glass bottles were filled from "lubesters" that held large quantities of oil. When cans became available, bottles were phased out, making them difficult to find and very collectable.

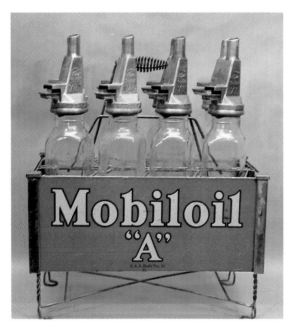

Mobiloil "A" eight "Filpruf" bottle rack, 1920s, eight quart bottles, with "Filpruf" pourers, Gargoyle logo. *Courtesy of Dunbar's Gallery.* $400-900.

Sunoco porcelain lighted bottle rack, circa 1925-1930, yellow with blue lettering, three eight-bottle wire racks, twenty-two bottles with fired-on Sunoco Logo, original spouts, 30" x 23" x 19" diameter. *Courtesy of Dunbar's Gallery.* Rare in complete condition, $1,000-2,000.

Four Shell 14" oil bottles, embossed with Shell logo, "Shell-Penn Motor Oil," "Shell Eastern Petroleum," and "100% Pennsylvania," 14" tall. *Courtesy of Dunbar's Gallery.* $25-60 each.

Four Sunoco one-quart oil, 9" bottles with painted labels, pourers, and caps, HM Co., complete with rack, 9" tall. *Courtesy of Dunbar's Gallery.* Scarce, $200-450.

Painted labels are harder to find and more valuable than those with decals.

Atlantic four-bottle rack, complete, has four one-quart, embossed glass, 9" bottles with pourers and caps, Atlantic logo on front, Atlantic Motor Oil on back. Bottles 14" tall. *Courtesy of Dunbar's Gallery.* $50-80 each.

Atlantic bottle details.

One Standard Iso-Vis 10" oil bottle complete with tin pour spout and cap. *Courtesy of Dunbar's Gallery.* $75-125.

Mobiloil rack with eight one-quart, glass, 6" jars, metal screw on covers, featuring Pegasus. *Courtesy of Dunbar's Gallery.* $100-200.

Details of Mobiloil A quart oil jar. $10-30.

Beacon oil bottles, lift-top rack with two labels, hinged lid with Penn Beacon Motor Oil logo labels, sixteen bottles, 11-1/2" x 18-1/2" x 13" diameter. *Courtesy of Dunbar's Gallery.* $200-600.

Veedol oil display rack, 52" tall. *Courtesy of Dunbar's Gallery.* $200-600.

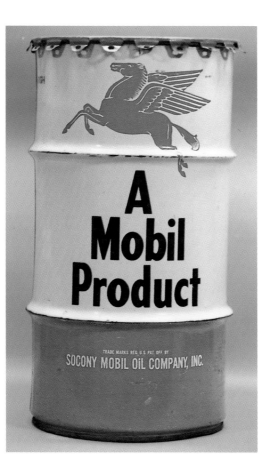

Mobil Oil drum, features Pegasus and "A Mobil Product" silk screened on enamel, 28" tall. *Courtesy of Dunbar's Gallery.* $200-400.

Mobiloil display rack, blue, four shelves, with enamel on steel sign, double Pegasus. *Courtesy of Dunbar's Gallery.* $200-400.

Atlantic Motor Oil rack, circa 1930s, embossed Atlantic on upper panel, 26" tall, with Wolf's Head cans. *Courtesy of Dunbar's Gallery.* Rack $100-350.

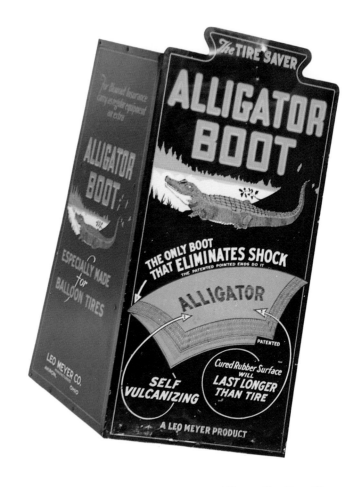

Shrader Tire Gauge tin counter display, 1930s, 18". *Courtesy of Dunbar's Gallery.* $200-400.

In sight, in the mind. Since the inception of service stations, oil and gas companies have sent advertising displays to promote their brands, making some garages look like a bewildering product wonderland.

Alligator Tire Boot litho on tin display, circa 1930s, three sides with alligator, 12" x 23" x 13". *Courtesy of Dunbar's Gallery.* $200-650.

Until the advent of radial tires, first released for sale by Michelin in 1949, drivers could plan on getting 10-15,000 miles from their rubber. However, with radial construction, the mileage vaulted drastically to 40-50,000 miles.

Bright Star Litho on tin counter display, circa 1930s, 20" x 6". *Courtesy of Dunbar's Gallery.* $100-250.

AP Mufflers tin display, "Don't Gamble with Dangerous Monoxide," 15" x 56" x 19". *Courtesy of Dunbar's Gallery.* $200-600.

These guys must have gotten their advertising tips from Ralph Nader.

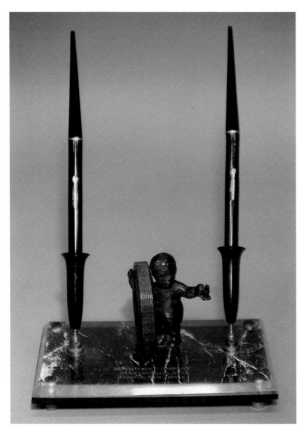

"United States Tires are Good Tires" figural, molded and pressed metal and glass spoked tire ashtray, circa 1920, with types of tires outlined at edge, 6" diameter. *Courtesy of Dunbar's Gallery.* Scarce, $100-300.

Fisk desk set, circa 1930, given to Roth Tire Co., marbeled base with pens, Fisk Boy. *Courtesy of Dunbar's Gallery.* $100-250.

Burma Shave wooden roadside sign, 40" x 11". *Courtesy of Dunbar's Gallery.* $100-300.

Early traffic control sign post from Goshen, New York, 57" tall including kerosene lantern, cast-iron, 17" diameter base, embossed "Traffic Sign" and "Signal Co. Gloucester, Mass," Pat. Jan 1916. *Courtesy of Dunbar's Gallery.* Scarce, $100-500.

Oilzum advertising materials packet, circa 1920, includes seven pages illustrating various advertising materials available to Oilzum dealers. *Bob & Judy Palmerino Collection, Courtesy of Noel Barrett Auctions.* $100-300.

Below: Automotive catalogues: Babcock Electrics, 1907, twenty pages, six full-page plates, 9" x 6", $75-200. Pope Waverly Electrics, 1906, twelve different autos, six commercial vehicles, 9" x 8", $75-200. Locomobile, 1906, thirty-six pages, five full pages of different models, 1" x 8". $75-200. All scarce. *Bob & Judy Palmerino Collection, Courtesy of Noel Barrett Auctions.*

Below: Assortment of automotive postcards, circa 1920s-30s. $1-10 each. *Bob & Judy Palmerino Collection, Courtesy of Noel Barrett Auctions.*

Below: Assortment of road maps, circa 1920s-30s. $1-10 each. *Bob & Judy Palmerino Collection, Courtesy of Noel Barrett Auctions.*

Chapter 3

Pinbacks

Used as dealer giveaways, the heyday of celluloid pinbacks mirrored the golden auto age, from the early 1900s just up to the Depression.

Celluloid, the first plastic synthetic material, began with French scientist Anselme Payeu and American counterpart Alexander Parkes, in the mid-1800s. John Wesley Hyatt obtained a patent for celluloid in 1869 and immediately put it to use. Its strength, colorability, and low cost made it a good substitute for ivory and other natural materials in such items as billiard balls, dentures, combs, brushes, and photographic film.

For the first time, voters in presidential campaigns of the late 1800s showed their allegiance on their lapel with celluloid pinbacks.

Whitehead and Hoag Company patented the celluloid button in 1896 and many companies followed suit. Buttons were produced plugging everything from holidays to shows to comic characters. For twenty-five years, celluloid dominated the button world.

However, celluloid has had one major drawback. If ignited, it burns ferociously. Film sometimes caused serious fires in movie theaters and hospital X-ray areas.

By World War II, celluloid gave way to tin buttons, which were cheaper to manufacture. Plastic was perfected and replaced celluloid in toys and other products.

Today the most valuable automotive-related pinbacks are those made for those early makes of cars only seen for a few bright years. Buttons that show the cars on them are worth more than those with only lettering.

Pinbacks are still a reasonably priced area for collectors, though this may change in the next few years. Beginners can still find buttons for just a few dollars, all the way up to several hundred dollars for the rarest examples in the best condition. One water or age spot or scratch makes a big difference in condition.

"The Most Beautiful Car in America - Paige" pinback with ribbon, circa 1920, 1908-1927, Detroit, Michigan, pin 1", ribbon 1-1/4". *Courtesy of Dunbar Moonlight Kid Auctions.* $50-125.
Paige cars were beautifully designed, sporty vehicles that used Duesenburg and Continental engines.

"Auto Speed Contest Racing" pinback, Aug. 21, 1904, St. Louis Fairgrounds Race Track, Steiner Badge Co., pin 1-1/4", ribbon 1-1/2". *Courtesy of Dunbar Moonlight Kid Auctions.* Very rare pin, $300-500.
This was supposed to be one of the highlights of the 1904 Worlds' Fair. Unfortunately, Barney Oldfield, one of racing's legendary figures, lost control of his vehicle and killed two spectators while injuring himself, the worst moment of his illustrious career.

1911 Brooklyn Automobile Show hat stud, embossed, 1" diameter, $50-150; and a 1914 New York Automobile Show figural stud, Mercury at the wheel, embossed, 3/4" x 1". *Courtesy of Dunbar Moonlight Kid Auctions.* $75-150.

Mercury was a popular figure used by Goodyear tires and the Ford company as the premier symbol of speed. Auto shows were effective in introducing new models to a large group of potential customers in a short period of time.

1909 New York AMCMA Auto Show stud pin, bronze, Whitehead & Hoag, stamped #3949 on reverse, embossed with mustached driver's profile bursting from wheel, 3/4" x 1". *Courtesy of Dunbar Moonlight Kid Auctions.* $50-100.

1917 Auto Show pinback, Torsch & Franz, Baltimore, Maryland, 1-1/4". *Courtesy of Dunbar Moonlight Kid Auctions.* $50-100.

Reverse of 1917 Auto Show pinback.

Browniekar, Omar Motor Co., Newark, New York, 1908-1910, Bastian Bros., Novelties, Rochester New York, 1-1/4". *Courtesy of Dunbar Moonlight Kid Auctions.* Scarce, $100-250.

The Browniekar was a light two seater, with a single cylinder, costing only $150 and intended mainly for children. The Kodak Brownie camera proved a better long-term investment.

"Own a Dort—You Will Like It" pinback, Dort Motor Car Co., Flint, Michigan, 1915-1924; Bastian Bros., Novelties, Rochester, New York, 3/4". *Courtesy of Dunbar Moonlight Kid Auctions.* $50-75.

Originally a carriage maker, Joshua Dort produced a Model 5 in 1915.

Montgomery-Ward 1898 electric buggy pinback, 1-1/4" diameter. *Courtesy of Dunbar Moonlight Kid Auctions.* $50-125.

Figuring that you would buy anything via department stores, this buggy was offered by M-W. Later on the company would continue to offer autos via the mail, including a 1913 Modoc for $1,250, bride not included.

Stanley Steamer pinback, circa 1910, F.E. Jens Co., 3/4". *Courtesy of Dunbar Moonlight Kid Auctions.* $75-150.

FE and FO, the Stanley twins, ran a photo plate business before venturing into autos, producing their first steam car in 1897. Steamers could outrun gas-powered cars. However, it took forever to warm them up. The production of Cadillac's self starter in 1912 pushed the Steamer into decline, although the company hung on until 1927.

Pair of "It's a Great Automobilie" Marmon Pinbacks, Nordyke & Marmon Co., Indianapolis, Indiana, 1902-1933, Whitehead & Hoag, Newark, New Jersey, both 1" x 1/2". *Courtesy of Dunbar Moonlight Kid Auctions.* $25-35 each.

Marmons were expensive—$5,000 for a 1921 touring car—and placed well in competition, but were another victim of the Depression.

Pair of moon pinbacks—Joseph W. Moon Buggy Co., Moon Motor Car Co., St. Louis, Missourri, 1905-1930; both made by Whitehead & Hoag. *Courtesy of Dunbar Moonlight Kid Auctions.* Motor Car pin: 1-1/2", $75-150; Buggy pin: 3/4", $50-75.

Louis Mooers shot for the top of the market, creating a 1926 auto named Diana, after the moon goddess, and the Prince of Windsor in 1929. Overreaching at the wrong time put the company out of business.

Oldsmobile figural stud, logo, circa 1910, 3/4". Paige figural stud, 3/4" long, circa 1912, $50-100. *Courtesy of Dunbar Moonlight Kid Auctions.*

Ransom E. Olds will be remembered for making the Curved Dash Runabout, the first mass-production automobile. In 1904, he left the company to found the Reo company. Reo's luxury market was snuffed by the Depression.

Me for an E-M-F '30' pinback, circa 1910, 1-1/4". *Courtesy of Dunbar Moonlight Kid Auctions.* Scarce, $50-100. A short-lived company, Everitt, Metger, and Flanders.

American Locomotive Motor Car pinback, Whitehead & Hoag, 3/4", $50-100. The MacArthur-Zollars Motor Co. Pinback, Whitehead & Hoag, 3/4", $50-100; American Six pinback, Bastian Bros., 3/4", $50-100; Studebaker Wagon pinback, Whitehead & Hoag, 3/4", $50-100. *Courtesy of Dunbar Moonlight Kid Auctions.*

Reverse of pinbacks showing Bastian Bros. and National Equipment Co. manufacturers' logos.

"Mora—The Sealed Bonnet Hero" pinback, circa 1910, Whitehead & Hoag, 1-1/4";
Moras were made from 1906-1910 in a variety of models, including the 145hp
Racytype, limited to 100 produced year; Rare, $100-250. "You Can Do It With A
Reo," Berwick Store Co. Pinback, Whitehead & Hoag, 1-1/4, $50-100; R. E. Olds
certainly did do it. After selling out his company to retire, a group of backers got
together and had him form another company, REO, which he ran until 1924,
realizing $50 million in sales, and he retired again, for good. McFarland Six
pinback, 1910-1928, circa 1915, 1-1/4", $50-100, Connersville, Indiana. McFarland
specialized in six-cylinder cars, making only a couple of hundred a year. *Courtesy of
Dunbar Moonlight Kid Auctions.*

Reverse of previous pinbacks.

"I Want a Maxwell" pinback, 1913-
1925, Detroit, Michigan, Whitehead &
Hoag, 1-1/4". *Courtesy of Dunbar
Moonlight Kid Auctions.* $50-100.

In 1913, Jonathan Maxwell
split with partner Ben Briscoe,
moved to Detroit, and started
building inexpensive cars. Walter
Chrysler took over the company in
1923 and it was completely
absorbed by 1926.

"The REO People" pinback, Fritz Bros. Auto Co., circa 1930, Whitehead &
Hoag, 1", $50-100; Rickenbacker Motor Co. pin, Detroit, Bastian Bros.,
Rochester, New York, 3/4", 1922-1927. Make sense of this—famed aviator
Eddie Rickenbacker made, in 1927, a car that was fast, high quality, unusual,
and priced low, and did not sell well. $75-150. Oak Motor Suits Pinback,
circa 1915; 3/4", $50-100. *Courtesy of Dunbar Moonlight Kid Auctions.*

Pilot pinback, Almy Auto Co., Distributors, Rochester, New York, Bastian Bros., 1-1/4". *Courtesy of Dunbar Moonlight Kid Auctions.* $75-150.

Pilot, of Richmond, Indiana, made functional and hardly decorative cars from 1909-1924, most with four or six cylinders. One year, 1916, buyers could order right- or left-hand steering, which was about as distinctive as Pilot would get.

Selden Car pinback, 1906-1914, Rochester, New York, Bastian Bros., 1-1/4". *Courtesy of Dunbar Moonlight Kid Auctions.* $50-100.

Selden private cars were discontinued in 1914, overshadowed by Model Ts, but continued commercial models until 1932.

Huber pinback, Marion, Ohio, circa 1910, Whitehead & Hoag, 1-1/2". *Courtesy of Dunbar Moonlight Kid Auctions.* $50-75.

"Buy a Moyer" pinback, H.A. Moyer Co., Syracuse, New York, 1911-1915, Bastian Bros., 1". *Courtesy of Dunbar Moonlight Kid Auctions.* $75-150.

Moyers were expensive, from $2,200 to $3,000, most with four-cylinder engines.

Overland pinback, Toledo, Ohio, 1903-1963, Bastian Bros., 1-1/2" x 1". *Courtesy of Dunbar Moonlight Kid Auctions.* $75-150.

Overland was a strong seller right before World War I. The 79 series sold 80,000 in 1914 at $950 each.

Overland figural celluloid stickpin, reverse side offers model for $1,075, circa 1920, Bastian Bros, 1-1/2" x 1". *Courtesy of Dunbar Moonlight Kid Auctions.* $75-150.

Overland offered styling, and value, which sold well in the 1920s, averaging 55,000-100,000 sales per year.

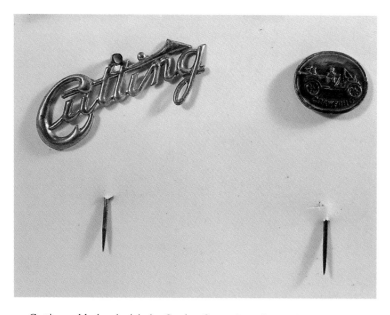

Overland Cars pinback, Oklahoma Car Co., Whitehead & Hoag Co., 1". *Courtesy of Dunbar Moonlight Kid Auctions.* $50-100.

The company Overland-Willys dropped Overland and started using theWillys name exclusively in the early 1930s, making a further name on Jeeps in World War I.

Cutting gold-plated stickpin, Cutting Carter Auto Co., Jackson, Mississippi, 1909-1913, 1-1/2"; Crawford Stickpin, embossed, 3/4". *Courtesy of Dunbar Moonlight Kid Auctions.* $50-100.

Cuttings ran in the first two Indianapolis races, in 1911 and 1912, but went out of business soonafter because of lack of funds.

Mitchell Six celluloid figural stickpin, 1-3/4" x 1/2" 1903-1923. *Courtesy of Dunbar Moonlight Kid Auctions.* $50-100.

Another wagon builder, Mitchell produced six-cylinder cars with torpedo-style bodies. A big mistake was using a sloping radiator in 1920, soon to be called the "drunken Mitchell." The resulting poor sales sent the company reeling. Nash bought the company in 1923.

Checker Taxi hat badge, circa 1923-present, Checker Cab Co., Kalamazoo, Michigan, G. Felsenthal & Sons, Chicago, 4-1/2" x 2-1/2". *Courtesy of Dunbar Moonlight Kid Auctions.* $25-50.

Mitchell stickpin, Mitchell Motor Car Co., Racine, Wisconsin, 1903-23, goldplated script, 1-1/2". *Courtesy of Dunbar Moonlight Kid Auctions.* $50-100.

Tourist tabbed pinback, Tourist Automobiles, 1902-1909, Los Angeles, California; Whitehead & Hoag Co., 1-1/4". *Courtesy of Dunbar Moonlight Kid Auctions.* $50-125.

Tourist came in five-passenger models and was the best known model of the West Coast at this time.

Pair of Dodge pinbacks, Dodge Bros., Detroit, Michigan: 1950 "Go with Dodge," 3". Dodge/Plymouth, 1-1/4". *Courtesy of Dunbar Moonlight Kid Auctions.* $5-20 each.

Dodges in the 1940s were hard to tell from their cousins, the DeSotos and Plymouths.

Fourteen Buick pins, 1903-1950s. *Courtesy of Dunbar Moonlight Kid Auctions.* $5-20 each.

Ten assorted automotive pinbacks, 1940s-50s: 1941 Plymouth and 1940 Plymouth, both 2-1/2", Cruver, Mfg. Co., Chicago. Lincoln-Mercury pinback with ribbon, 2". Lincoln oval, 2-1/2" x 1-1/2". Pontiac, 1-1/2". 1949 Nash Airflyte, 2-1/4". "You Certainly Auto" 2". Genereux Motor Co., French, 1-1/2". Relay Motor Trucks, 1-1/2". Chevrolet "Start the New Year Right," 2". *Courtesy of Dunbar Moonlight Kid Auctions.* $5-20 each.

Twelve Chevrolet pinbacks, 1911-1940s. *Courtesy of Dunbar Moonlight Kid Auctions.* $5-20 each.

Three 1930s Chevrolet pinbacks. *Courtesy of Dunbar Moonlight Kid Auctions.* $5-20 each.

Reverse of "I'm Voting for Chevrolet" pinback, 1937, Geraghan Co., Chicago, 1-1/4". *Courtesy of Dunbar Moonlight Kid Auctions.*

Reverse of Chevrolet pinbacks "C Day Is Coming," L.J. Imber Co.

Ten Studebaker pinbacks. *Courtesy of Dunbar Moonlight Kid Auctions.* $5-25 each.

Ford pinback, 1", circa 1915. *Courtesy of Dunbar Moonlight Kid Auctions.* $50-125.
   Half a million Americans showed their smarts in 1916, buying Model T Fords in utilitarian black.

Five Pontiac and Oakland pinbacks: "It's Spring," 1", Greenduck Co., Chicago. "For Economy and Riding Comfort," 3/4". "It's Spring," 1", Greenduck Co., Chicago. Oakland with shield, 1-1/4". "For Economy and Performance," 1". *Courtesy of Dunbar Moonlight Kid Auctions.* $25-50 each.

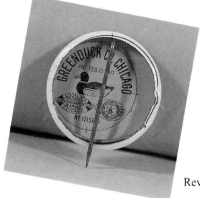

Reverse of Ford pinback.

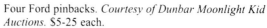
Four Ford pinbacks. *Courtesy of Dunbar Moonlight Kid Auctions.* $5-25 each.

Three Ford pinbacks. *Courtesy of Dunbar Moonlight Kid Auctions.* $5-25 each.

Two Plymouth-Chrysler pinbacks. *Courtesy of Dunbar Moonlight Kid Auctions.* $10-40 each.

Two Willys pinbacks. *Courtesy of Dunbar Moonlight Kid Auctions.* $50-100 each.

In 1915, the company was close to the top, second only to Ford in sales. In 1916, Willys-Knight was the first auto company to offer automatic windshield wipers as standard equipment on its touring model.

Cadillac pinback, Sidles Garage
Co., Lincoln, Nebraska, 1-1/4".
*Courtesy of Dunbar Moonlight
Kid Auctions.* $25-75.

Diamond T Motor Trucks pinback, 1905-1911,
1". *Courtesy of Dunbar Moonlight Kid
Auctions.* $50-75.
   *Diamond T made large cars with four-
cylinder motors. Diamond T commercial
trucks are still made today.*

Chevrolet Sales Convention pinback, 1-1/2"; $5-25. Hudson
stickpin, 1" triangle x 2-1/2" long, $10-40. *Courtesy of Dunbar
Moonlight Kid Auctions.*

Paterson "30" celluloid mirror, circa 1910, WA
Paterson Co., Flint, Michigan, 1908-1923, 2-3/4"
x 1-3/4". *Courtesy of Dunbar Moonlight Kid
Auctions.* $50-150.
   *Another buggy company changing over
to gas power, Paterson made primarily four-
and six-cylinder autos.*

Selection of thirty-one early pinback buttons. *Bob & Judy Palmerino Collection, Courtesy of Noel Barrett Auctions.*
1) The Maxwell, "Perfectly Simple-Simply Perfect", 1" oval, $75-125
2) Detroit Electric, dated 1910, 1-1/4", $75-125
3) Cutting, Runabout with driver, 1911-1912, 1" oval, $50-100
4) The White, early buddy style car, 1-1/4", scarce, $50-150
5) Implement and Vehicle Dealers Association, dated 1910, 1-3/4", $75-150
6) Hupmobile, dated 1911, 1-1/5" oval, $100-200
7) Expo-Auto and Truck Show, dated 1912, 1-1/4", $100-250
8) Pair of 1909-1912 pinbacks, $25-75; Winton Six, 1-1/4", scarce, $75-150
9) Franklin Field Day, dated 1910, 1-3/4", $75-150
10) Stanley Steamer, 7/8", circa 1910, $75-150
11) Firestone Columbus, 1907-1915, 1", scarce, $100-200
12) Boss Steam Car, 1903-07, 1-1/4", rare, $150-300
13) Velie, Moline, Illinois, circa 1910, 1-1/4", $75-150
14) Stephens, circa 1920, 1-3/4", $100-300
15) Elmore, dated 1907, 7/8", scarce, $75-150
16) The Lambert, circa 1912, $75-150
17) Knox, 1909 Models, 1-1/4", $75-175
18) BrownieKar, 1-1/4", $100-200
19) Velie Auto 40 Pin, 2", Velie Auto 30, 1", $75-150 each
20) Atlas Runabouts & Touring Cars, Havens Motor Car., Denver, 7/8", $75-175
21) Bridges Motorcar and Rubber Co., 1", $75-150
22) The Canadian Crow, 1-1/4", $25-75
23) Wyckoff-Cord Auto Co., Sioux City, Iowa, 1-1/4", $75-150
24) 1911 Cadillac 30, 1.5", $100-200
25) Pittsburgh Six, 1901-1911, 3/4", rare, $50-100
26) Premier-Patterson Co.,circa 1910, 7/8", $75-150
27) Indian Motocycle Agent, circa 1912, 1-1/4", $150-350
28) Another Nash, circa 1920s, 1-1/4", $75-150
29) Scout-American, American Motors, circa 1912, 1-1/4", $75-150
30) Milwaukee, dated 1901, 7/8", rare, $100-300
31) Motor Car Magazine, dated 1912, 1-1/2", scarce, $50-100
32) The Imp, Denver dealer, 1913-1914, 1-1/4", $75-150
33) Montgomery Ward Electric Horseless Carriages, 1-1/4, $50-125
34) The Davis, circa 1914, Richmond, Indiana, 1-1/4", $50-125
35) Minneapolis Auto Show, 1907, 1-1/2", scarce, $100-250

Selection of twelve early pinback buttons, circa 1910-1930s. *Bob & Judy Palmerino Collection, Courtesy of Noel Barrett Auctions.* $10-30 each.

105

Twenty pinbacks and pins: Overland, Nash, Hudson, circa 1910-1940s. *Bob and Judy Palmerino Collection, Courtesy of Noel Barrett Auctions.* Early pinbacks with auto images, $50-100 each; others $10-30.

Thirty-three pinbacks, 1915-1960s. *Bob and Judy Palmerino Collection, Courtesy of Noel Barrett Auctions.* Early pinbacks with auto images, $50-100 each; others $10-30.

Eighteen lapel pins and studs, most enamelled brass, early 1900s. *Bob and Judy Palmerino Collection, Courtesy of Noel Barrett Auctions.* Early pinbacks with auto images, $30-100 each.

1 & 2) Mason pinbacks, 1906-1910, $50-100 each
3) Elkart pinback with ribbon, 1908-1909, rare, $50-150
4) Velie Limited, 2-1/4", $50-150
5) Austin Bantam, 2" Dia., 1901-1921, $50-150
6) The Gearless Car, 2-1/16", 1907-1909, $50-150
7) Fordson Farm Tractors, 1-3/4", $50-150
8) Cartercar Motor Co. 1906-1916, $50-150
9) Van Brunt Vehicles with Ribbon, 2-1/4", ribbon 4-1/2" long, rare, $150-300
10) Graham Paige button with ribbon, $50-150
11) Three pins and ribbons to identify salesmen at automobilie shows, Fiat, Lozier, Palmer, and Singer, 2-3/4", $50-100 each
12) Carhart Motor Co., Overland & Willys, 2-1/4", $100-200

Eleven badges, employee and police, for Reo, Cadillac, Chevrolet, Humber, Ford Plant Protection Badges (these were usually thugs hired by Ford management to quell any union talk), enamelled brass, 1920s-30s. *Bob & Judy Palmerino Collection, Courtesy of Noel Barrett Auctions.* $20-50 each.

Kelly Springfield playing cards with image of lotta miles inside tire, that pneumatic nymph of the 1920s. *Bob & Judy Palmerino Collection, Courtesy of Noel Barrett Auctions.* $100-200.

Celluloid Pocket Mirrors. *Bob & Judy Palmerino Collection, Courtesy of Noel Barrett Auctions.*
1) Pullman Automobilies, 1903-1917, 2-1/4", $100-250
2) Lexington-Davis Automobile Sales Co., 1909-1928, 2-3/4" x 1-3/4", $100-250
3) Alpena Motor Cars, 1910-1914, 2-3/4" x 1-3/4", $100-250
4) Stevens-Duryea Six Cylinder, 1902-1927, 2-3/4" x 1-3/4", $100-250
5) Marion Bobcat, 1904-1914, Marion, Indiana, $100-250
6) Wood Electrics, 2-1/2", 1899-1919, $50-125
7) Durant, 1921-1932, 2-3/4" x 1-3/4", $100-250
8) Elmore, 1900-1912, 2-3/4" x 1-3/4", $100-250
9) Demotcar, 1909-1911, $50-125
10) Paterson 30, 2-3/4" x 1-3/4", $50-150
11) Owen, Wiles Motor Co., Ford Dealer, 2-3/4" x 1-3/4", $50-150
12) Stutz Ideal Motor Car Co., 1911-1935, 2", $100-250
13) Dodge Brothers Coupe, 1-3/4", $30-75
14) Mahlke Automobile Garage, 2-3/4" x 1-3/4", $25-100
15) Apperson, Kueffer, 1902-1926, 2-3/4" x 1-3/4", $100-200
16) Oakland- Maxwell-Reo, 2-3/4" x 1-3/4", $100-250
17) Mack Truck paperweight mirror, 2-1/2", $100-350

1) Maccar Truck Sales Co. paperweight mirror, circa 1920, 3-1/2", $100-250
2) Ludlow Ambulance Service paperweight mirror, 3-1/2", $50-125
3) Yellow Taxi Co. paperweight mirror, circa 1920s, 3-1/2", $100-300
4) Yellow Cab cap badge, $25-50
5) Yellow Cab glass paperweight, 2-1/2" x 1-3/4", $100-150
6) Euclid Automobile Co. celluloid note case, 1907-08, Cleveland, Ohio, $100-200
7) Auburn Beauty Six celluloid note case, 1921 calendar on reverse, 3-3/4" x 2-1/4", $100-200
8) Jacob Reed's Sons celluloid covered automobile record books, 3-3/4" x 2-1/4", $25-75
9) Jenny Gasoline safety razor in case, 4" x 2", very unusual premium, $150-350
10) Jenny Gasoline playing cards complete deck, circa 1930s, $100-200
11) Maxwell Automobiles tip tray, 4-1/4", circa 1914, $75-150
Bob & Judy Palmerino Collection, Courtesy of Noel Barrett Auctions.

---

1) 1930s-40s Esso sterling letter opener, $100-200
2) Pair of Bowser & Hayes (gas pump makers) letter openers, 1920s, 9" long, $50-100 each
3) Oakland letter opener, circa 1920, 9" long, $50-75
4) Burrelle Automobiles, brass, circa 1920, 9" long, $50-75
5) Chevrolet , 1949, bronze, 9" long, $50-75
6) Monogram Oil letter opener, bronze, 9" long, $50-75
7) Detroit Springs, 9" long, $50-75
8) Weber Implement & Auto Co., 9" long, $50-75
9) Mohawk Gasoline paperweight, copper-flashed bronze, 3-1/4" diameter, $200-400
10) Dort Advertisng paperweight, $50-150
11) Dort pinback on felt pennant, $50-100
12) Aluminum with paper pad hanging calendar, $50-100
13) Two Vermont Car for Hire registration plates, cast brass 1917 and 1918, $100-200 each
Bob & Judy Palmerino Collection, Courtesy of Noel Barrett Auctions.

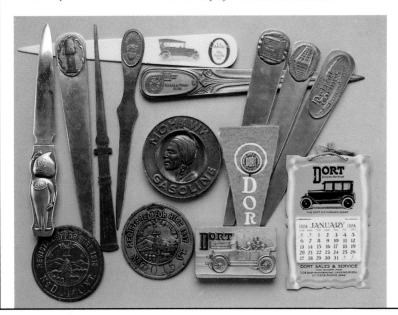

1) Fisk Tire rubber and glass ashtray, circa 1920s, 6-1/2" diameter, $50-75
2) Fisk blotter, 6" x 3-1/2", $10-30
3) Fisk postcard, 1911, 6" x 3 1/2-, $10-20
4) Buick advertising compact, 1930s, 2" diameter, $100-150
5) Chrysler advertising compact, 1930s, 2" diameter, $100-150
6) Advertising Tops, including Chalmers Six, Elgin & Apperson, Earl Motor Car, Norse Oil Co., 1910-1920, $20-40 each
7) Railway Express Agency badge, enamel and brass, 2" x 2", $100-!50
8) Embossed Buick leather paperweight, 3-1/4" diameter, $50-75
9) Buick pocket mirror, 2-3/4" x 1-3/4", $50-75
10) Buick brass stickpin, $50-75
11) Buicks metal ashtray, $50-75
12) Chevrolet leather wallet, $50-75
13) Chevrolet tape measure, $25-50
14) Pair of Corvette gas caps, $200-250 pair,
Bob & Judy Palmerino Collection, Courtesy of Noel Barrett Auctions.

Chapter 4

Cast Iron Toys

When windmills were created way back, forged cast iron was not far behind. Stronger than tin, iron served as the choice for railroad tracks, ships, and tools, helping to jumpstart the Industrial Revolution.

In the United States, mechanical and still banks were made in the 1870s to promote thrift after the Civil War. Horse-drawn toys followed, and, when the horseless carriage made its appearance, it was only a matter of time before its image would be molded in diminutive form. The automotive cast iron heyday would be parked in two decades.

Arcade made its first cast iron Yellow Cab in 1921. Stock sold out immediately. Rival cast iron toy companies such as Kilgore, Hubley, Kenton, and Dent, worked quickly to develop their own automotive and truck lines.

They advertised their new wares as "They Look Real" and "They're Different." Cast iron toys were both. Manufacturers signed up for exclusive rights to copy distinctive models, which helped to produce a built-in audience. Companies such as Arcade Manufacturing of Freeport, Illinois, and Hubley Manufacturing of Lancaster, Pennsylvania, worked different sides of the miniature street. Arcade captured Ford, Chevy, Reo, Mack, and International. Hubley grabbed Packard, Borden's, Elgin, and Bell Telephone.

In the 1920s, while the stock market soared like a giddy balloon, Gershwin composed Rhapsody in Blue, flappers danced, Al Capone sold black-market booze, Fibber McGee and Molly entertained, and the Algonquin Round Table spoofed the high life, little kids were rolling out their Ford Flivvers and Mack Dumptrucks, dreaming about life off the farm.

Arcade and Hubley expanded their factories. The good times seemed endless ... until the Depression closed down the party. Sales dropped, toys became more worn as money was portioned to food first. FDR pushed the New Deal, millions ate at soup kitchens, Dillinger holed up at his dad's, Dizzy Dean pitched for the St. Louis Cardinals, Joe Louis boxed, and much of the country watched Shirley Temple for escape from the new dreary era.

Toy companies had to adjust fast, shrinking their lines in size and scale, augmenting with NDQ (nickel, dime, quarter) toys that sold more easily. Gone were the huge gas and coal trucks and vans and big expensive cars—just like the disappearance of their dads' fancy vehicles.

Some toy companies turned to other businesses. Others, like Arcade and Hubley, survived the Depression, but not World War II. The hopelessnes of the Depression was stamped out by the will to win the war, once the country was dragged in by Japan's raid on Pearl Harbor. Now steel and iron were needed to build full-size vehicles to transport soldiers in Europe and Asia. Scrap drives reposessed many a cast iron coupe in the name of patriotism.

After the end of World War II, cast iron equaled dinosaur. Cheaper wind-up tinplate toys had also been developed in the 1920s and plastic was just a Tupperware party away from popularity. Kenton made a few cast iron toys in the 1950s before closing its doors. Hubley made diecast toys. Arcade was gone.

Forty years later, big boys and girls seek out examples for their own collections. What to look for? Toys with all original paint and parts and with no repairs will be more costly than those that have been restored. Larger models tend to bring more money because they were more expensive at the time of the original sale (from 5 cents to $2!). The level of paint makes the largest difference—the spread between a toy with 90 percent and 98 percent paint could be double! Average prices for the NDQ toys are $50-300, with exotic short-lived pieces reaching $500-700. Large trucks sell between $600-3,000 depending on the models. The rarest of the rare taxicabs, cars, and trucks bring up to $10,000. One Arcade showroom model Yellow Cab with a sample tag sold at auction several years ago for $60,000, a record. That is beyond the high end.

This great sprawling value spectrum is why you will see such wide price ranges in this book. Beginning collectors must understand (if I haven't repeated myself enough in this book) that **condition means everything**. Say it in the morning, say it in the evening, say it when someone dangles a toy in front of you with half its paint worn off and says, "It's in the book for $500—I'll sell it to you for $300." Yeah, maybe it's listed at $500 with 85 percent paint. That's why you have to educate yourself, to know what's a fair deal.

What's the future for cast iron toy collecting? Well, as long as new collectors enter, this category will thrive. When a number of collectors get older and decide to sell their collections, it generally excites active collectors and the publicity entices new collectors. Conversely, collectors tend to collect what they had as children. Boomers are collecting more comic character toys and games. With an average price of $100-500 a toy, there has to be a strong pull to become a collector in cast iron toys.

This means that the market will probably appreciate slowly and steadily, just as it has done over the past twenty-five years, unless a public figure (like a Cosby, Forbes, or Winfrey) choose to collect. Then, it will skyrocket for a couple of years, then calm down again.

Finally, beware of crummy reproductions from Taiwan and China. These should be easy to differentiate—they tend to be much heavier than the originals. They are also poorly molded, with few details, and are dipped in a heavy, gaudy, bright coat of paint.

Arcade cast-iron Chevy Superior Utility Coupe, circa 1925, 7" long. *Courtesy of Dunbar's Gallery.* Scarce model in rare dark green color, $200-900.
Notice the differences between the two Chevy coupes. Customers were learning that they didn't have to look exactly like their neighbor and their kids soon found the same thing out in their toys.

Arcade cast-iron gas pump, circa 1930s 4 1/2" tall. *Courtesy of Dunbar's Gallery.* $100-300.
By the 1930s gas pumps were a familiar sight. Of course, the government soon jumped on the bandwagon and instituted the first federal gas tax in 1932, the first in the world.

Arcade cast-iron Chevy Superior Utility Coupe, circa 1925, 7" long. *Courtesy of Dunbar's Gallery.* Scarce model, $200-900.
In 1925, Arcade added Chevrolet to its growing stable of real-life auto lines. The company helped by working with Arcade to make the miniatures faithful in looks, adding such nice details as the Chevy bowtie logo stamped on the radiators and spare tire holders.

Arcade cast-iron Model "T" Coupe, circa 1925, red, 6-1/2" long. *Courtesy of Dunbar's Gallery.* $200-800.

Arcade took some license here, as from 1913-25 Henry Ford only allowed black Model "T"s. However, with its increasingly outdated look and slumping sales, Ford succumbed, offering colors in 1926. This toy color variation is also hard to find.

Arcade cast-iron Buick Sedan, circa 1928, 8-1/2" long. *Courtesy of Dunbar's Gallery.* $1,000-4,000.

Six years after offering its first automotive toy, a Yellow Cab, Arcade had grown to be the number one cast-iron toy maker in America by 1927. Through aggressive advertising and product development and design, Arcade had momentarily cornered the market in cast-iron toys. Again, Arcade signed up the Buick division and offered a pair of handsome Buick sedan and coupe models. This and the following sedan are shown for their difference in options. The red (a much rarer color) Buick has nickel-plated wheels, which are more popular with collectors, as they do not deteriorate. However, rubber tires were more popular with moms, as they caused less damage to floors and counters and were much quieter. The coupe (not shown here) is rarer than the sedan.

Arcade cast-iron Buick Sedan, circa 1928, 8-1/2" long. *Courtesy of Dunbar's Gallery.* $1,000-4,000.

Arcade cast-iron Chevy Coupe, circa 1928-29, 8" long. *Courtesy of Dunbar's Gallery.* $500-2,500.

A must car in every good collection for its classic lines and great styling. The 1920s could be thought of as the "rolling '20s" as more than 20 million Americans owned cars. Alfred Sloan of GM, in developing his auto hierarchy, saw that cars were becoming part of the owners' identity. He spent more on design, and, as a result, overtook Ford in sales in 1927, partly thanks to the popularity of this coupe, which sold for about $600. It even received front-wheel brakes in 1928 and a spiffy new motor, nicknamed the "Cast-iron Wonder," in 1929. Arcade sold many copies of this coupe to the kids of the parents who had one in their newly built garage. Most are found in this grey and black, although other colors (red, green, and blue) were offered in the Arcade catalogue at a lesser price. The other color variations, are rarer and worth more.

Hubley CI open roadster, circa 1930s, nickel grille, 6" long. *Courtesy of Dunbar's Gallery.* $150-500.

While Arcade dominated most of the auto line, Hubley concentrated on racers, airplanes, and motorcycles. Therefore, many of Hubley's toy cars are not affiliated with any auto makers and are an amalgam of design and imagination.

Hubley cast-iron station wagon, circa 1930s, 6" long. *Courtesy of Dunbar's Gallery.* $300-1,000.

This model looks very much like the famed Ford Model A "Woody" wagons. At this time, station wagons were still in their infancy—a marriage of delivery truck and automobile. In the early 1930s, Ford began offering a Model A wood-bodied wagon, usually made with birch or maple. Originally the bodies were done by the Mingel Co., until 1935 when Ford started buiding the wagons at its plant in Iron Mountain, Michigan, with its nearby hardwood forests. Ford usually sold between 3,000-10,000 "Woody" wagons a year during the Depression. Almost all auto makers would offer station wagons by the 1950s, when housewives needed them to cart the kids and groceries to and from their homes in the newly created suburbs.

Hubley CI Woody station wagon, circa 1930s, 6" long. *Courtesy of Dunbar's Gallery.* $300-1,000.

For their unique looks and large capacity, not to mention the Beach Boys, at times woody wagons have caught the public's nostalgic imagination. Not many toy versions were made, however.

AC Wiliams cast-iron take-apart sedan, circa 1930s, 7" long. *Courtesy of Dunbar's Gallery.* $200-600.

AC Williams was involved in the cast-iron toy and bank business from the early 1900s through 1938. Known for inexpensive toys, its products were sold mainly through five and dime stores such as Woolworth's. Their line was generic but nicely designed and offered an alternative to those who couldn't afford the fancier and larger Arcade and Hubley models. AC Williams examples can usually be distinguished by the metal hubs used with its white rubber tires. The company still exists, having switched to industrial castings during World War II.

112

AC Wiliams cast-iron sedan, circa 1930s, 7" long. *Courtesy of Dunbar's Gallery.* $200-600.

Notice the differences in the spare tire and the molding, as this model is a one-piece casting.

Pair of AC Williams CI take-apart blue coupes circa 1930, 4-1/2" long. *Courtesy of Dunbar's Gallery.* $50-150.

Take-apart toys were popular because kids could interchange chassis and bodies to make different combinations, some of which were sold in kits of cars and trucks.

Hubley cast-iron #602 Coupe, 6" long, circa 1930s. *Courtesy of Dunbar's Gallery.* $200-600.

By the late 1920s, automobile styling had moved from the primitive and functional to the golden age, with glamorous flowing lines. Although this toy is a small casting, it's three colors, has nice detail, and a nickel grille to make it quite desirable.

Hubley cast-iron low-slung touring car, circa 1930, 5-1/2" long. *Courtesy of Dunbar's Gallery.* $100-500.

Note the great running boards, which died out with World War II, a favorite of machine gun toting cops and robbers.

Pair of Kilgore cast-iron take-apart coupe and sedan, circa 1930s, 4" long. *Courtesy of Dunbar's Gallery.* $50-200.

Like AC Williams, Kilgore, of Westerville, Ohio, made mostly NDQ toys (nickel, dime, quarter) that were often sold in sets. Kilgore is also known for its line of cap pistols. The company was probably a corporate casualty of World War II. While some company's thrived taking on government orders, other companies, because of materials shortages, had no supply and just ceased to exist.

Arcade cast-iron Pierce Silver Arrow coupe, circa 1936, 7" long. *Courtesy of Dunbar's Gallery.* $200-600.

 With a stunning sleek design and a 175 hp motor that could speed to 115 mph, the long front end pointed to a fine future during its display at the 1933 Chicago World's Fair. But, a $10,000 price tag during the height of the Depression aimed straight at distaster, which is why only 5 Silver Arrows were made and sold. Arcade made many more toy replicas of this car, which proved far more popular. The toy version, like its real-life counterpart, has become a classic.

Hubley CI Livery Car, circa 1936, 7" long. *Courtesy of Dunbar's Gallery.* Scarce, $200-600.

 Livery carriages and limousines have been around as long as there have been customers willing to be to be driven from Fancy Ball A to Fancy Ball B. This Hubley version uses the same body as for its Yellow Cab. Note the painted driver and passenger—it's a rare car.

Hubley CI Lincoln Zephyr, circa 1935, nickel grille, 7" long. *Courtesy of Dunbar's Gallery.* $300-900.

 Lincoln was Henry Leland's second auto company—his first was Cadillac. However, he ran into some financial problems and sold out to Henry Ford in 1922. It was Ford's prestige market response to Cadillac and Packard. However, luxury sales in the 1930s were as few and far between as mink stolls. Lincoln developed the Zephyr, which was designed better than the Airflows. It was lighter, but its unibody structure, which was also far less expensive, allowed it to be far more durable in crashes. Morever, it sported a beefy V12 engine and sold in huge numbers, making Lincoln a player.

Hubley Deco Coupe, circa 1936, 6" long. *Courtesy of Dunbar's Gallery.* $200-500.

 This car was a portent of 1950s styling, low and wide. This vehicle is a combination of any number of luxury cars, a little bit Auburn boat tail, a little bit Cord body, a little Duesenberg, a little Chicago Century of Progress.

Hubley cast-iron Chrysler Airflow, circa 1934, 7-1/2" long.
Courtesy of Dunbar's Gallery. $500-1,800.

Chrysler engineers got the idea of creating an aerodynamic car in the late 1920s. Walter Chrysler okayed his engineers to build a car using aircraft principles. The result was the Airflow line, which featured radical rounded lines, a "waterfall" radiator, a roomier seating compartment, and great speed performance, setting more than seventy records. Model lines Chrysler, Plymouth, and DeSoto sported versions, which were released late in June 1934. In the meantime, rumors circulated that the car was a lemon. Publicity could not stop the snowball effect or combat the public's apathy to the new look. Funny that thirty years later, a similiar looking Volkswagen Beetle would capture a place in the American public's heart.

Hubley cast-iron Chrysler Airflow, circa 1934, 6"
long. *Courtesy of Dunbar's Gallery.* $200-600.

Walter Chrysler liked innovation, which is why he gambled on the Airflow line. Chrysler was the first auto company to offer a padded dashboard in 1949, and a hi-fi in-dash record player in 1956 as a special option. Unfortunately, one also had to order special size records.

Hubley cast-iron Airflow, circa 1934, 6-3/4" long. *Courtesy of Dunbar's Gallery.* $200-500.

Like Walter Chrysler, Hubley bet on the Airflow toy line, with mixed results. However, these cars are highly collectible today.

Arcade cast-iron Yellow Cab, circa 1920s, 9" long. *Courtesy of Dunbar's Gallery.* $200-800.

From the early 1900s to 1921, Arcade Mfg. Co. of Freeport, Illionois, had a nice business making cast-iron still banks, horsedrawn vehicles, and toy kitchen items. In 1921, Arcade entered an agreement with the Yellow Cab company to make a miniature replica Yellow Cab. The cab was a huge hit, starting a run of several years where Arcade could do no wrong. Arcade's strategy coincided with the good times of the 1920s. They made exact reproductions of fullsize cars with the blessing of the auto companies. Arcade advertised heavily in publications such as Playthings, ran toy fairs that introduced new models, and made themselves the number one cast-iron toy maker in the United States by 1927. Arcade reached its apex in the late 1920s. The company spent much money on expanding its production capabilities and on producing expensive larger toys. When the Depression hit, Arcade was much slower to respond than rival Hubley, taking several years of poor sales before it revamped its line with smaller, cheaper toys. By 1943, Arcade was out of gas, shut down, and sold to Rockwell-Standard Co., a foundry that made aircraft engine pistons. The golden era of cast-iron toys was over, and one of its two kings ended its reign.

Cast-iron Airflow, circa 1934, 6-3/4" long. *Courtesy of Dunbar's Gallery.* $200-500.

Other toy companies made versions of the airflows. This one has a fully molded body, without the distinctive nickel radiator.

Arcade Cast-iron yellow cab, circa 1920s, 5" long. *Courtesy of Dunbar's Gallery.* $200-800.

    With the success of the original 9" Yellow Cab, Arcade chose to create other variations. This smaller 5" size, known as the No. 3 cab, made in the mid 1920s, is more difficult to find than the larger 8" counterparts.

Arcade cast-iron flat-top Yellow Cab, circa 1928, 8-1/2" long. *Courtesy of Dunbar's Gallery.* $800-2,000.

    Reflecting the updated design, Arcade made this model, listed as No. 5 Limousine Yellow Cab in its catalogue and ads, but known as the Flat Top among collectors. It came with nickel headlights mounted on the windshield posts. This a much harder to find and fancier taxi than the regular Yellow Cab. Arcade began to put decals on its vehicles in 1928. Each vehicle is embossed Arcade in the underside of the body.

Kenton cast-iron Liberty Cab, curved windshield, circa 1925, 5-1/2" long. *Courtesy of Dunbar's Gallery.* Scarce, $200-1,000.

    This is a variation of the sedan model made by Kenton that year. Like Arcade and Hubley, Kenton enjoyed enormous success in the 1920s, with a toy line of 500 different models encompassing autos, cap pistols, still banks, and trains. By the end of the decade, though, Kenton was scrambling with its brethren to stay in business, cutting its toy line in half.

Freidag cast-iron Yellow Cab, circa 1920s, 8" long. *Courtesy of Dunbar's Gallery.* $500-1,200.

    Freidag was based in Freeport, Illinois, and, like neighbor Arcade, produced a line of cast-iron toys. However, the company did not last long and Freidag toys are considered scarce and desirable.

Arcade cast-iron Ford Taxi, circa 1933-34, 6-1/2" long. *Courtesy of Dunbar's Gallery.* $400-1,800.
  Made as a souvenir of the Chicago World's Fair. The extra stencilling and association give it more value.

Hubley cast-iron Yellow Cab, circa 1930s, 7" long. *Courtesy of Dunbar's Gallery.* $400-1,000. This is an unusual version without the lights and taxi sign.

Hubley cast-iron Sky View Yellow Cab, circa 1930s, 8" long. *Courtesy of Dunbar's Gallery.* $400-1,000.
  Sky view taxis had sunroofs, so the passengers could gaze happily into the heavens, ignoring the running meter.

Kenton cast-iron Fire Chief's Open Roadster, circa early 1920s, 6" long. *Courtesy of Dunbar's Gallery.* Scarce, $400-1,000.
  In the early 1900s, Waterous Fire Engine Works of St. Paul, Minnesota, manufactured the first motorized fire pumper with a single engine that could both power the vehicle and drive the water pump. Replicating the products of daily life, toy companies soon followed suit and made a whole line of fire vehicles, from pumpers to ladder trucks to fire chief's personal cars.

Arcade cast-iron Fire Chief's Model A Coupe, circa 1927, 6-1/2" long. *Courtesy of Dunbar's Gallery.* Scarce, $500-1,500.
  These coupes were produced for a short period of time, known as doctor's coupes, and discontinued when the Model A hit the showrooms. In red and stamped Fire Chief, it is a doubly rare example.

Kenton cast-iron Fire Hose Truck, circa 1920s, 6-3/4"
long. *Courtesy of Dunbar's Gallery.* $300-700.
    *Nickel wheels with painted inserts were a
hallmark of Kenton in the 1920s.*

Kenton cast-iron Fire Chief's Coupe, circa 1933, 5-1/2"
long. *Courtesy of Dunbar's Gallery.* Scarce, $400-900.

Kenton CI Patrol Wagon, circa 1927, nickeled solid wheels
with red centers, 9" long. *Courtesy of Dunbar's Gallery.*
Scarce, $500-1,500.
    *In 1922, the Denver Police Department bought
the first specially made police car. Called a bandit-
chaser, it featured a Cadillac motor and a bullet-proof
body. However, it had no roof or doors! It was ready
to rumble, however, stocked with rifles, searchlights,
and a machine gun mounted on the hood. The rear
seats were higher than the front so the police in back
could see over (and presumably avoid shooting off)
the heads of those in front.*

Dent cast-iron Police Patrol with box, circa 1920s,
6-1/2" long. *Courtesy of Dunbar's Gallery.* $300-
900.
    *You can see from the look of the truck
that it's a transitional vehicle in the
changeover from oat-fed horsepower to gas-
fed horsepower. Found brand new in its
original box, it's possible that this was put
together from parts found in the factory years
after it had closed down. Then again, maybe
it just sat in someone's attic. Dent, of Fuller-
ton, Pennsylvania, produced high quality
original-design cars and trucks in the 1920s,
discontinuing toy manufacture in the early
1930s.*

118

Hubley cast-iron Fire Ladder Truck, circa 1930s, 9" long. *Courtesy of Dunbar's Gallery.* $200-500.

Ladders on fire fighting equipment were introduced in the 18th Century. The first successful aerial ladder truck was invented in 1868 by Daniel Hayes, a San Francisco fireman. The ladders were self-contained, readily extendable, and could be directed at almost any angle toward a burning building, something that was not possible with the older types of ladders. Modern fire engines use hydraulic ladders that can rotate on a disk.

Arcade cast-iron Andy Gump Car, circa 1920s, 7-1/4" long. *Courtesy of Dunbar's Gallery.* $800-2,000.

Following the success of the Yellow Cab series, Arcade licensed popular comic strip dad Andy Gump and built him a hot little 348 roadster. Hugely popular, Andy remained in the Arcade lineup until 1931. Surprisingly, there were no other character cast-iron motor vehicles until the

Cast-iron Toy Trucks

Hubley cast-iron 5-Ton Delivery Truck, 1920s, 17-1/2" long. *Courtesy of Dunbar's Gallery.* $500-1,500.

With its early headlamps, this was one of the first cast-iron transitional vehicles, from horsedrawn to motorized, and one of the largest. Therefore, examples will be found occasionally with a crack in the iron chassis or with the tailgate missing. Kids loved this truck. It was so popular that Hubley sold the 5-ton model all through the 1920s, even as they sold more modern designs.

Arcade cast-iron Model A Cab with two trailers, circa 1929-31, side dump: 13-3/8" long, and stake body trailer: 11-1/4" long. *Courtesy of Dunbar's Gallery.* Rare, $500-1,500.

In the 1870s, steam-powered vans made deliveries. The first truck powered by Karil Benz's gas engine was made by German engineer Gottlieb Daimler. In 1903, the newly formed Automobile Club of America ran the furst U.S. commercial vehicle contest to test the economy, reliability, durability, speed, and carrying capacity of the truck. Promotion and attention from the contest propelled the growth of the trucking industry. By 1908,

4,000 trucks were hauling freight on crude U.S. roads. World War I boosted the use of trucks even more, when 250,000 were aquired for the U.S. effort in Europe. By 1918, more than a million were truckin'. Toy trucks were just a length behind and in full force by the mid 1920s.

AC Williams CI Tractor with Stake-side Trailer, 7" long. *Courtesy of Dunbar's Gallery.* $100-300.

Early trucks were very heavy and their mechanics crude. Tractor trailers were first used just after World War I, their advantage being that the back end could be detached and the tractor used to haul another trailer while the first was being unloaded.

Arcade cast-iron Ford Stake Truck, circa late 1920s, 8" long. *Courtesy of Dunbar's Gallery.* $200-500.

With the advent of motorization, trucks cut the time of deliveries and cars allowed people to run more errands, go more places, pursue more interests. Automobiles helped to usher in the era of instant gratification. Most of the toy trucks built in the 1920s either resembled Fords, Macks, or a designer's whimsy.

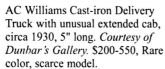

AC Williams Cast-iron Delivery Truck with unusual extended cab, circa 1930, 5" long. *Courtesy of Dunbar's Gallery.* $200-550, Rare color, scarce model.

Yellow just wasn't used a whole lot on cast-iron toys, particularly on trucks.

Hubley cast-iron Bulldog Mack Stake Truck, circa 1920s, 4-1/2" long. *Courtesy of Dunbar's Gallery.* $50-150.

Hubley, of Lancaster, Pennsylvania, was the yang to Arcade's cast-iron yin. Hubley's motto was "They're Different" in response to Arcade's "They Look Real." Founded in the 1890s, Hubley began making cast-iron toys in the teens. It found its niche in cast-iron automotive toys after World War I. With the rise of brand names in the 1920s, Hubley traveled a slightly different road from Arcade, concentrating on exclusive rights deals with motorcycle makers Harley-Davidson and Indian, as well as product lines such as Bell Telephone, Borden's, and Old Dutch Cleanser, molding a distinct identity from Arcade. Its trucks often had the C cab Mack look to them.

AC Williams cast-iron Stake Delivery Truck, circa 1930, take-apart chassis, 6-1/2" long. *Courtesy of Dunbar's Gallery.* $100-400.

In 1915, most trucks still did not have roofs, doors, and windshields. By 1930, however, most cabs were completely enclosed, thereby protecting drivers from the weather and other drivers.

Champion cast-iron Mack Stake Delivery Truck, circa 1930s, 7-1/2" long. *Courtesy of Dunbar's Gallery.* $200-450.

Champion Hardware Co. of Geneva, Ohio, made cast-iron parts for other companies in the 1920s. When other companies succumbed to the Depression, Champion began its own line of cast-iron toys which continued to 1936, when the company returned to its original hardware manufacture. Many of Champion's toys were painted dark blue. Its motorcycle line was very popular. Most Champion toys are embossed with the company name.

Hubley cast-iron 10-Ton Stake Delivery Truck, circa 1938, 8-1/2" long. *Courtesy of Dunbar's Gallery.* $200-450.

Hubley survived the Depression well, changing much of its toy line to inexpensive models (like this truck) sold in department stores. Like so many other businesses, Hubley took on war contracts during the second world war and never went back to making cast-iron toys.

Hubley cast-iron Railway Express Delivery Truck, circa 1930s, 5" long. *Courtesy of Dunbar's Gallery.* $100-350.

This truck was part of the Hubley NDQ line (nickel, dime, quarter) but still has an affiliation with one of the leading trucking companies of the 1930s.

Hubley cast-iron Motor Express Delivery Truck, circa late 1930s, 8" long. *Courtesy of Dunbar's Gallery.* $200-550.
This was one of Hubley's last designs, keeping pace with continual modern style changes.

Arcade Mack ice truck, circa late 1920s, 10-1/2" long. *Courtesy of Dunbar's Gallery.* $500-2,000.
This truck is hard to find with the original tongs and ice. Mack Trucks, Inc. was founded in 1905. Motorized trucks had preceded autos by several years. Mack built trucks, tractors, and trailers. The Mack C cab design of the 1920s was used by many toy makers, although only Arcade had the official Mack license. Known as the "bulldog" for its toughness and durability, Mack adopted the pooch for its mascot. Now a subsidiary of Renault, Mack still builds tough trucks.

Arcade Mack Ice Truck, circa 1930s, original ice, tongs, and box, 7" long. *Courtesy of Dunbar's Gallery.* $500-1,500.
Even rarer than finding the tongs and ice is finding an original box, which can double the value of a toy.

Arcade White Ice Truck, 1939, original ice and tongs, 6-3/4" long. *Courtesy of Dunbar's Gallery.* $200-500.
In the fledgling refrigeration industry, ice manufacture was needed. However, after the proliferation of electricity and the development of air conditioning, the refrigerator began to replace the icebox and put thousands of icemen out of jobs by the late 1930s.

Arcade Cast-iron International Red Baby Dump Truck, circa 1928, working crank-up dump lift mechanism, rubber tires, nickel driver, decals, 10-1/2" long. *Courtesy of Dunbar Moonlight Kid Auctions.* $500-900.

This International Harvester Dump Truck, better known as the Red Baby, features a crank and pulley system to raise and lower the dump body for hours of fun. Founded by Cyrus McCormick and originally known for their reapers and farming equipment, International Harvester branched out in the 1920s, developing a full line of delivery and construction vehicles.

Arcade cast-iron Mack Dump Truck, circa 1925, working hoist, 12" long. *Courtesy of Dunbar Moonlight Kid Auctions.* Scarce color, $500-1,500.

When Arcade promised that the toys would "look real," they also meant that they'd work for real, too. This was Mack's answer to the International. Early versions did not have Mack embossed on the doors.

Arcade Cast-iron Mack High Lift Coal Truck, circa 1925, with working lift mechanism, rubber tires, nickel driver, embossed Mack on cab doors, 10" long. *Courtesy of Dunbar Moonlight Kid Auctions* Unusual truck, $500-2,000.

Another great truck that actually lifts and dumps! This model was only made 1931-33. In 1932 fake coal was given as a promotion. Finding that with one of these examples would raise the value.

Kilgore cast-iron Mack Dump Truck, circa 1920s, 8" long. *Courtesy of Dunbar's Gallery.* $200-500.

Kilgore's slogan was "Toys that Last" and cast-iron toys did, absorbing much wear from a generation that had very few playthings. It's amazing that so many of these toys have survived in this good shape. Remember, the amount of paint is a huge determining factor in the value of a toy. A rare toy with little or no paint is often no more valuable than a common toy with exceptional paint.

Hubley Mack Dump Truck, circa 1920s, 8-1/2" long. *Courtesy of Dunbar's Gallery.* $200-1,000.

Even with the establishment of the auto and trucking industry, the U.S. govenment did not start to seriously try to improve and build roads until the The Federal Highway Act of 1921, which provided for primary highway routes across the length and breadth of the nation. Even the new construction of this period was virtually confined to roads serving expanding communities. The post World War II building boom pushed families to suburbs outside the cities and forced the govenment to build roads to carry those families back and forth.

Hubley 6-Wheel Tandem Dump Truck, circa 1940, 7-1/2" long. *Courtesy of Dunbar's Gallery.* $100-400.

Another one of Hubley's last toy models. At this point, it's easy to see that the golden age of design is truly over.

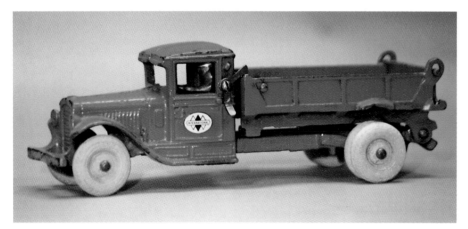

Arcade International Dump Truck, 1930s, original white rubber tires, dual wheel rear end, 11" long. *Courtesy of Dunbar's Gallery.* Rare, $500-2,000.

This truck was a part of an International series that Arcade offered in the mid-1930s. Other models included a panel delivery truck in green and a stake truck in red. All are very difficult to find. This may be because they did not sell well or were made in smaller numbers than earlier models.

Arcade Lubrite CI Gas Truck, circa late 1920s, 12-1/2" long. *Courtesy of Dunbar's Gallery.* Scarce, $700-2,000.

The first gas delivery vehicles were horsedrawn. With the proliferation of gas stations and demand, major companies soon invested in their own fleet of gas trucks. These miniatures were among the heaviest and most popular of the Arcade line (and the most expensive). Lubrites were special-order trucks.

Arcade CI Gas Truck, 1928, red, nickel driver, decals, stencilled "American Oil Co.", 12-1/2" long. *Courtesy of Dunbar's Gallery.* $700-2,000.
Oil companies would sometimes letter toys and use them for promotions.

AC Williams Mack Gas Truck, circa 1928, 7" long. *Courtesy of Dunbar's Gallery.* $200-400.

Hubley Gas Truck, circa 1938, 7" long, stamped "Texaco." *Courtesy of Dunbar's Gallery.* Unusual, $100-500.
Probably a promotional toy special ordered by Texaco. By the late 1930s, toys were a lot less fancy.

Arcade Mack "C" Cab cast-iron wrecker, circa 1930, 12" long. *Courtesy of Dunbar's Gallery.* $800-2,500.
The largest and hardest to find wrecker in the Arcade series. Sold for $2 in stores.

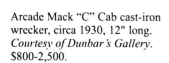

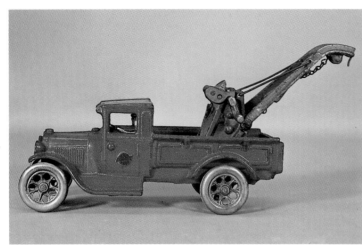

Arcade cast-iron Model A Weaver Wrecker, circa 1928, red, nickel wheels and driver, 11" long. *Courtesy of Dunbar Moonlight Kid Auctions.* $300-1,000.

    When the Model A finally came out in 1928, both Ford and Arcade used it in as many variations as possible to make up for the time the plant was closed for retooling. This size was the second largest and retailed for $1 in 1930.

Champion Bulldog Mack C Cab Wrecker, circa 1930s, 7" long. *Courtesy of Dunbar's Gallery.* $100-500.

Hubley Wrecker, circa 1930s, 6-3/4" long. *Courtesy of Dunbar's Gallery.* $100-400.

    My dad drove a wrecker for years and, subsequently, collected the cast-iron toy versions. At one time he had twenty-six different examples, most in this condition, played with, but still bright.

Hubley take-apart wrecker, circa 1930s, 7" long. *Courtesy of Dunbar's Gallery.* $100-400.

    This toy went with an open roadster, coupe, and truck that could all be mixed and matched.

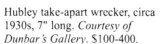

Champion Mack C Cab Wrecker, circa 1930, 8-1/2" long. *Courtesy of Dunbar's Gallery.* $100-400.

This was Champion's largest wrecker.

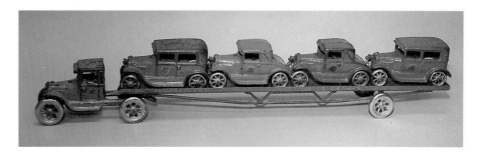

Arcade Model A Car Carrier, circa 1930, 24-1/2" long, with two Model A Coupe and two Model A Sedans. *Courtesy of Dunbar's Gallery.* $1,000-2,500.

As of 1920, America had 3 million miles of highway, with only 36,000 miles paved with an all-weather surface that could support automobiles. By the end of the 1930s, an interstate highway system was in process, making it easier for car carriers like this to deliver the goods.

Hubley CI Nucar Transport Car Carrier, circa 1938, 16-1/2" long, excellent condition, includes three vehicles: 1934 Hubley CI Open Wrecker; 1936 Hubley Chrysler Air Flow two-door coupe; 1932 Hubley Sport Roadster. *Courtesy of Dunbar's Gallery.* $800-2,000.

AC Williams Car Carrier, circa 1930s, 12-1/2" long. *Courtesy of Dunbar's Gallery.* $300-600.

Arcade Car Carrier, circa 1938, 16" long. *Courtesy of Dunbar's Gallery.* $400-1,000.

Please note the brightness of the original toy. Many of the toys featured in this book are of this quality, putting them on the high side of the estimates.

Arcade White Moving Van, circa 1928, Lammert's of St. Louis, Missourri, 13" long. , *Courtesy of Dunbar Moonlight Kid Auctions.* Rare, $5,000-10,000.

This is one of Arcade's scarcest and most sought-after toys. A promotion for Lammert's Furniture of St. Louis, this van is also found lettered for other companies, costing almost $2 retail.

Hubley Borden's Milk delivery truck, circa 1930, 5-1/2" long. *Courtesy of Dunbar's Gallery.* $500-1,500.

Borden's milk hails back to the Western pioneer days. Gail Borden, who settled in Texas, invented a process for preserving milk by boiling and evaporating it and sealing it in a closed container. Used by the U.S. Army during the Civil War, his condensed milk became widely popular because it was safe and had a long shelf life, unlike the unpasteurized milk then available. The New York Condensed Milk Co., founded by Borden in 1858, still exists today as Borden's, Inc.

Arcade cast-iron Hathaway Bread International Delivery Truck, circa 1930, 9-1/2" long. *Courtesy of Dunbar's Gallery.* $500-2,500.

A great promotional truck that's very hard to find in great condition.

Kenton CI Overland Circus "Bear Cage" Truck, circa 1927, 9" long, drop-down back door. *Courtesy of Dunbar's Gallery.* Scarce, $500-2,000.

Another toy that's very hard to find in better condition than that portrayed in the photo. President Lewis Sharps (LS) Bixler was the president and guiding force behind Kenton's success in the 1920s. He designed this very unusual cage wagon as well as a circus motorized calliope that's also very rare. There are no other toys quite like these examples.

Hubley CI Bell Telephone Truck, circa 1930s, 9" long. *Courtesy of Dunbar's Gallery.* $500-1,500.

This toy was a kid's delight. An auger, ladders, post, and tools made for hours of playtime. Hubley sold tons of these toys and you can see them at shows, in five different sizes, with this the largest. As you can imagine, it's not very easy to find this fully equipped. The largest size featured tools that actually work.

Hubley Bell Telephone Truck, circa 1930s, 3-1/4" long. *Courtesy of Dunbar's Gallery.* Very scarce size, $100-400.

Hubley CI Bell Telephone Truck, circa 1930s, 5" long. *Courtesy of Dunbar's Gallery.* $100-400.

Kenton cast-iron Galion Master Road Roller, 7-1/2" long, original box. *Courtesy of Dunbar's Gallery*. $300-800.
This toy was probably made during Kenton's last years, the late 1940s-50s.

Kenton CI Jaeger Cement Mixer, 7" long. *Courtesy of Dunbar's Gallery*. $200-450.
This was one of Kenton's biggest sellers, which is why you see them at every toy show today.

Hubley cast-iron Bulldog Mack C Cab General Steam Shovel, circa 1930, 10" long. *Courtesy of Dunbar's Gallery*. $300-800.
The first steam shovels were used in the 1830s to excavate land for railroads. Using the Hubley toy versions, kids could dig their own land for mini roads, driveways, or mini malls.

Hubley CI Huber Roadroller, circa 1920s, 7-1/2" long. *Courtesy of Dunbar's Gallery*. $200-600.
The Huber Co., of Marion Ohio, produced farming and construction equipment, such as threshers, tractors, and road rollers. Horsedrawn rollers were originally used in England in the early 1800s, laying down macadam roads of condensed stone. Look at the detail in the casting Hubley used to recreate the actual steam roller— everything but a working engine.

Hubley CI Huber Roadroller, circa 1920s, Hubley decal, 7-1/2" long. *Courtesy of Dunbar's Gallery.* $200-600.

Kenton cast-iron Cement Truck, with Jaeger Sidedump Mixer, circa 1930, 8-1/2" long. *Courtesy of Dunbar's Gallery.* Scarce, $500-2,000.

This combination of Kenton motorized truck with side dump is extremely rare.

Kenton cast-iron Jaeger Cement Mixer Truck, circa 1930, 9-1/2" Long. *Courtesy of Dunbar's Gallery.* Scarce in this larger size, $500-2,000.

Kenton cast-iron Jaeger Cement Mixer Truck, circa 1930, 7-1/2" long, with original box. *Courtesy of Dunbar's Gallery.* $400-900 (Add $500 for box).

Dent cast-iron Road Scraper, circa 1930, 5" long. *Courtesy of Dunbar's Gallery.* $50-150.

Chapter 5

Miscellaneous

A Marriage Made in the Backseat, Or Rock 'n' Roll Dreaming

"Safety—Our Children Please!" porcelain sign, double sided, circa 1930s, 20" x 30". *Bob & Judy Palmerino Collection, Courtesy of Noel Barrett Auctions.* Scarce, $300-900.

In the early 1960s, Ralph Nader forced the U.S. government to take a look at the auto industry as a result of his complete disenchantment with the Chevrolet Corvair, which, with its rear engine, had poor handling characteristics. Because of Nader's efforts to improving safety, Congress passed the National Traffic and Motor Vehicle Safety Act in 1966. For the first time, car design was placed under federal control and safety standards were mandated for all motorized road vehicles.

Someday someone is going to come out with a book on collectible car radios. After all, there has been a longstanding marriage between music and motoring since the first aftermarket radios developed by Motorola in the 1920s. I think that it's no coincidence that the development of America's highways in the 1950s helped pave the way for the rise of rock 'n' roll.

When radio took to the airwaves in the 1920s and '30s, you could only drive around as fast as the smoothness of the roads let you.

The car was another crazy new fangled technological contraption to get used to, and it wasn't always reliable, safe, or fun, unless your idea of a good time was being stuck in a rumble seat in the rain. (which it could've been) So, no matter how much you were swinging to Benny Goodman

and Duke Ellington in the Big Band era, rocks, potholes, and cows provided loud and dangerous percussion. Anyway, that music was for dancing and spooning, not for driving. Jitterbugging and slow bumping and grinding provided the entertainment and mating calls for the pre-World War II years.

For the parents in the Depression generation, the car was an expensive means of transportation, shortening the distance from Point A to Point B. Very few kids were allowed the luxury of driving when eating was a priority.

With the advent of better roads, bigger and cheaper cars, and the newfound wealth and confidence that winning World War II brought to post-war America, people opened their eyes and pocketbooks wide and decided to take a spin to check out the scenery beyond their back door. In 1951, lots of people liked Ike because he and Congress appropriated more than $1 billion to improve the country's highway system. In 1955, lots of people under 30 fell under the spell of Elvis, letting their legs and pelvis swing to the beat of Hound Dog, Jail House Rock, Love Me Tender and other hits.

These new rock 'n' roll songs (whitewashed versions of longstanding black rhythm and blues) jumpstarted teens, who learned a whole new sport called "cruisin." For $5 or $10 you could buy a used DeSoto or Hudson, eke out $1 or $2 for gas, and take to the streets (when you weren't back in the garage trying to get it running). Your chaperones for the evening were Elvis, Buddy Holly, Chuck Berry, Little Richard, and Bill Haley among others.

After all, rock 'n' roll is about freedom and rebellion,

American Central Insurance Co., brass sign, circa 1920, St. Louis, embossed with Pierce Arrow Limousine, 14" x 10". *Courtesy of Dunbar's Gallery.* $300-1,000.

In 1906 the first stolen car was reported. Since then, many more cars have made one way trips to malls, parking lots, and curbs, and many agents have built lovely homes made of premiums. Automobile insurance takes up a hefty part of a multi-billion dollar industry. This sign is great and unusual— incised brass with a lovely etched auto. Without the car, the sign would only be worth a third, maybe, at the most.

Aetna Auto Assoc. porcelain diecut sign, double sided, circa 1920s, 20" x 14". *Courtesy of Dunbar's Gallery.* $200-500.

Some insurance companies have performed double duty, offering services beyond policies. Unfortunately, no company has managed to stop the close to 1.7 million auto thefts that occur each year (for you stat junkies, about one every 19 seconds) or the 45,000 auto fatalities that happen annually on our highways, or the 25,000 car jackings that have suddenly become a new national sport.

---

as well as being black slang for sex. It's about being different from one's parents. Well, that's the way it was in the 1950s and '60's. Now we all listen to oldies stations, even though most of us are out of the house and maybe parents ourselves.

Songs about driving seemed to come into vogue in the 1960s. The Sultans of Surfing, the Beach Boys, were also the Kings of Cruising. We could ride in our "Little Deuce Coupe" or have have "fun, fun, fun" until Daddy took our T-Bird away. The Beatles even invited us for a spin—"She's Got a Ticket to Ride" and "Baby You Can Drive My Car."

Then the '70s brought us the very obvious "Making Love in My Chevy Van," which kind of summed up the history and purpose of Back Seat Music. This brings us back full circle to the vision of Richie Cunningham falling out of the front seat of his sedan while in the arms of some *tart de jour* with a jaunty pink scarf around her neck (probably to hide anticipated hickies).

In the '80s, color was in with "Pink Cadillac" or "Little Red Corvette."

We don't have enough space to discuss country driving songs. After all, every other country song concerns a pickup truck, a six pack, and a lost love, a very dangerous combination for those crossing the street ahead. As much as I love the Judds and Conway Twitty, I'll let the *Four Wheel Drive Gazette* handle this weighty topic.

I've always found that driving and music combine my two favorite forms of escape. I still take to the streets when I need to get away and think. Singing and moving gives me the illusion of going forward and leaving my problems behind, even if they reappear at my door a few hours later. It's intoxicating, but legal, spiritual but down to earth. Just give me a song with a good beat and let me go.

And think about it—where could you have romance in high school, besides Mrs. Kowalski's couch, when she and Mr. Kowalski were snoring off their chipped beef dinner? In the car. How many days and nights do you spend commuting to and from work, Little League games, dancing

lessons, dentist appointments, and malls? How many hours at traffic lights? There would be far more violence in this country if someone hadn't figured out a way to stick Marconi's invention in the dashboard.

My teenage years were 1975-79, the disco era, which I tried to ignore. I flipped the radio station every time I heard a high-pitched voice squeaking out "Staying Alive." Working in a junkyard, I had my pick of cars, but chose a 1970 Oldsmobilie Cutlass two-door hardtop as my first. Orange with a black gut and white vinyl hat, I could not keep a low profile (I'm wondering if it was a special Halloween model), but I didn't care. It had an automatic transmission and a 455 motor, Oldsmobile's most powerful engine. Dual ex-

Massachussets State Auto Association/AAA porcelain sign, circa 1920s, stamped "Balt. Enamel", 23" x 13". *Courtesy of Dunbar's Gallery.* Scarce, $200-600.

Founded in 1902, the American Automobile Association (AAA) has helped motorists chart their trips and find clean hotels and good food since the hand crank starter. Over the years, the organization has become a federation of local automobile clubs, with a total membership well over 30 million. AAA also works to improve roads, and offers cheaper flights, legal aid, insurance, and emergency road services for its subscribing travelers.

---

hausts gave it a husky throaty sound, which I pushed at every red light.

My best friend Marcia and I spent many evenings leaving our boyfriends behind, just picking a direction and driving. We loaded up the eight track (talk about collectibles) with Steely Dan's "Aja" or Carly Simon's "Boys in the Trees" and just drove, past churches, Dairy Queens, town halls, reservoirs, high schools, and endless fields. It was our own personal constant music video. Occasionally we would meet up with admiring (sometimes of the car, sometimes us, sometimes both) men, who we always called Poindexters. We would politely accept accolades for the hot wheels, talk a little bit about its specs, then make our getaway when asked about our own.

Steely Dan was not for sharing or for mindless conversation. We were young, but we had a quite a streak of street smarts for two small town girls. We knew what we wanted, and more importantly, what we didn't want. It wasn't until later in life that we let our men into our cars, tape decks,

and hearts, and only the really special ones.

Today, I listen to a little bit of everything, from Louis Armstrong to Frank Zappa, the Sherrelles, Rondells, and any other good sounding -ells, NPR news and some kick ass country. But when I really need a moment to relax and reflect, I pop Steely Dan into the CD player, rev up the GMC Jimmy (oh, how times have changed), pop open the sunroof, and let Deacon Blues wash over me like a warm whirlpool. I know that music will be with me in sickness and health, in good times and bad, for ever and ever. Amen.

Federal Hi-Way Tourist Guide porcelain sign, double sided, 30" x 24", $100-300. Automobile Blue Book porcelain diecut shield sign, 1922, 21" x 19", rare, $200-600. *Bob & Judy Palmerino Collection, Courtesy of Noel Barrett Auctions.*

Tourism was not an industry until the advent of the railroad and the Industrial Revolution. By the 1920s, however, with centuries of pent up longing and a Tin Lizzie in hand, thousands took to the mostly unpaved roads in search of a little adventure. To protect unsuspecting tourists from dishonest operators, a number of organizations sprung up offering guidebooks that listed places that met the standards required. Businesses wanted their names in these books, as it gave them instant credibility and therefore increased their profits. Sometimes this attention was earned, sometimes it was bought, much like most political systems.

Royal Auto Club Hotel porcelain sign, double sided, 18" square, $100-300; Massachusetts Garage Association porcelain diecut shield sign, 24" x 24", rare, $300-1,000. *Bob & Judy Palmerino Collection, Courtesy of Noel Barrett Auctions.*

Automotive Maintenance Association of Sacramento, porcelain diecut sign, 20" x 18", $200-600. Organized Master Auto Repairmen porcelain sign, double sided, circa 1930, 18" x 18".*Bob & Judy Palmerino Collection, Courtesy of Noel Barrett Auctions.* $200-500.

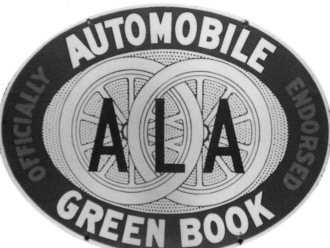

ALA Green Book porcelain sign, circa 1920s, 23" x 17". *Courtesy of Dunbar's Gallery.* $150-400.

Notice the interlocking spoked wheels, a tipoff that it's a 1920s sign. At this time there was a green book, a blue book, and a red book, all for identifying credible garages and hotels. Notice the absence of a black book, used for listing other types of endorsements.

Danger, Sound Klaxon wooden sign, circa 1920, 25" x 19", $100-300. Overland Co. Garage tin sign, circa 1915, 25" x 13". *Bob & Judy Palmerino Collection, Courtesy of Noel Barrett Auctions.* Scarce, $200-600.

The first auto horns were the clown type, and had to be used sparingly, because they upset horses, who were still used to being king of the road. As traffic increased, horns, like other safety features, were further developed and integrated into the mechanical systems. Some more trivia: Frederick Converse, the first American composer to have an opera performed at the Metropolitan Opera House, achieved far more notoriety with his 1927 orchestral piece, Flivver Ten Million, in which he included a wind machine and an auto horn to celebrate the production of the ten millionth Ford car.

National Commercial Travelers Association porcelain sign, double sided, 15" x 18". *Courtesy of Dunbar's Gallery.* $100-300.

New Hampshire AA tin flange sign, black & white, wheel shaped, 18" x 13". *Courtesy of Dunbar's Gallery.* $100-350.

Mexican AMA porcelain sign, 23" x 17". *Courtesy of Dunbar's Gallery.* $100-200.

With more than 3.5 million cars, trucks, and motorcycles driving in Mexico City, the AMA has its hands (and roads) full.

AAA Touring Information Board porcelain sign, 21" diameter. *Courtesy of Dunbar's Gallery.* $100-300.

Mass. Division AAA Emergency Service oval porcelain sign, double sided, 29" x 23". *Courtesy of Dunbar's Gallery.* $100-200.

For some reason, motorist organization signs have never really been highly collected, so prices have remained fairly low, except for really early, graphic, rare signs. Until they are discovered, it's a good way for beginning collectors to start without having to spend a lot of money per sign.

Emergency ALA Service porcelain sign, double sided, 20" x 18". *Courtesy of Dunbar's Gallery.* $100-200.

IGO Member enamel on steel sign, circa 1950s, double sided, 30" x 30". *Courtesy of Dunbar's Gallery.* $50-150.

Motor Stop porcelain sign, early sign circa 1920, Stonehouse Steel Sign Co., Denver, 14-1/2" x 6". *Courtesy of Dunbar's Gallery.* $100-300.

Organized Master Auto Repairmen porcelain sign, double sided, circa 1930, 18" x 18". *Bob & Judy Palmerino Collection, Courtesy of Noel Barrett Auctions.* $200-400.

Rand McNally Official Hotel porcelain diecut sign, double sided, circa 1930s, 14" x 17". *Bob & Judy Palmerino Collection, Courtesy of Noel Barrett Auctions.* Great graphics, scarce, $500-2,000.

This is one of the most beautiful and dynamic automotive signs ever made and is desirable for its artistic merits as well as its scarcity. Rand McNally, known for atlases, also rated travel services such as hotels and restaurants. In 1952, highway culture (a term used loosely) was completely redefined when the first Holiday Inn opened its green and white doors, eventually becoming the world's largest motel (motor hotel) chain.

Assorted porcelain signs: No Parking, 14" diameter, $75-150. Limousine Stand, 11" x 14", $75-150. Autos, 12" x 8", $100-200. ARO Specialized Lubrication, 21" x 6", $75-150. Standard Oil Co. Truck Sign, 10" x 13", scarce, $300-600. Sound Klaxon, 20" x 7-1/2", $100-400. Casgrain Speedometer, 12" x 6", scarce, $200-800. *Bob & Judy Palmerino Collection, Courtesy of Noel Barrett Auctions.*

Pony Express Trail porcelain sign, 14" diameter. *Courtesy of Dunbar's Gallery.* $200-500.

This sign commemorates the short-lived (1860-61) Pony Express mail service. Its route started in Saint Joseph, Missouri, and extended 2,000 miles to Sacramento, California. It was not financially successful and was discontinued when telegraph lines were set, but the route later became a road enjoyed by a new type of rider.

NOTICE
FILLING SERVICE
WILL NOT BE RENDERED
WHILE MOTORS ARE RUNNING,
OCCUPANTS SMOKING
OR LAMPS BURNING.

Filling Service porcelain sign, circa 1920, 12" x 10". *Courtesy of Dunbar's Gallery.* Scarce, $100-400.

What happens when gasoline is ignited? It explodes inside your engine, pushing the power to your drivetrain. What happens when gasoline is ignited outside your engine? It explodes, pushing the power of flames to your feet and making you run, fast. This is the simple evolution of the service station no smoking sign. Once completely unpopular and inexpensive, "No Smoking" signs have been hot lately, with prices doubling and tripling for early station-affiliated signs. With the notation of "lamps burning," it's obvious that this is a very early sign, and therefore, collectable.

Fire Use Only porcelain sign, 24" x 4". *Courtesy of Dunbar's Gallery.* $25-75.

Fire Extinguisher porcelain sign, 24" x 4". *Courtesy of Dunbar's Gallery.* $25-75.

Danger porcelain sign, 14" x 10". *Courtesy of Dunbar's Gallery.* $50-175.
Did the surgeon general write this?

Positively No Smoking, porcelain sign, 20" x 7". *Courtesy of Dunbar's Gallery.* $1000-4,300.

Please Do Not Smoke porcelain sign, 12" x 6". *Courtesy of Dunbar's Gallery.* $50-150.

No Smoking porcelain sign, 14" x 10". *Courtesy of Dunbar's Gallery.* $50-150

NO SMOKING

No Smoking porcelain sign, 18" x 5-1/2.
Courtesy of Dunbar's Gallery. $50-100.

No Smoking porcelain sign, 12" x 8".
Courtesy of Dunbar's Gallery. $50-150.

NO SMOKING

No Smoking porcelain sign, 24" x 4".
Courtesy of Dunbar's Gallery. $25-75.

No Smoking porcelain sign, 18" x 7".
Courtesy of Dunbar's Gallery. $50-150.

NO SMOKING
BY ORDER OF THE STATE FIRE MARSHAL

Texaco No Smoking porcelain sign,
circa 1950s, 22" x 4". *Courtesy of
Dunbar's Gallery.* $100-300.

No Smoking porcelain sign, 12" x 4".
Courtesy of Dunbar's Gallery. $25-75.

Texaco No Smoking porcelain sign, 1960 logo, 23" x 4". *Courtesy of Dunbar's Gallery.* $75-200.

Signs that are affiliated with a station are more valuable than those that aren't.

Union 76 Stop Your Motor porcelain sign, double sided, 30" x 6". *Courtesy of Dunbar's Gallery.* $200-600.

#35 Mobil No Smoking tin sign, single sided, oil/gas with dual Pegasus, 18" x 4". *Courtesy of Dunbar's Gallery.* $10-20. This is a reproduction!

Cities Service Clean Restrooms porcelain sign, circa 1950s, double sided, 22" x 24". *Courtesy of Dunbar's Gallery.* $200-400.

Restroom signs, like no smoking signs, were ignored for a long time. It has only been in the past couple of years that collectors decided that they had some value and prices have steadily risen. Cities Service used a black logo in the 1930s, switching to green in the 1950s.

Mobilgas dealer porcelain pledge sign, "To Provide Clean Restrooms," 7-1/2" x 7-1/2". *Courtesy of Dunbar's Gallery.* $100-500.

Gas and grease jockeys didn't have the white glove touch when it came to keeping restrooms sparkling. However, by the late 1930s, the larger companies in particular made an effort to offer clean facilities with results that have been, in my experience, uneven at best.

Sunoco Rest Rooms porcelain sign, withwrought iron bracket, circa 1940, 21" x 6-1/2". *Courtesy of Dunbar's Gallery.* $200-500.

One wouldn't expect a speck of filth or grime to infiltrate a restroom watched over by such a gentile couple. The original iron bracket adds about $100.

THE NEXT USER OF THIS REST ROOM WILL APPRECIATE YOUR COOPERATION IN HELPING US KEEP IT AS CLEAN AS POSSIBLE

HUMBLE

Humble Oil Co. porcelain restroom sign, Humble Oil Logo. *Courtesy of Dunbar's Gallery.* $100-300.

It's hard to find anything with a Humble or Esso logo.

CLEAN REST ROOMS

WINDSHIELD SERVICE

A Sinclair Dealer Service

Sinclair Clean Rest Rooms double sided porcelain sign, 30" x 37". *Courtesy of Dunbar's Gallery.* $200-400.

If this sign had a man with a cap or an auto, the price would go up considerably. Graphics mean so much in a sign's value.

MEN LADIES

Pair of Cities Service Men/Ladies porcelain flange signs, 15" x 5". *Courtesy of Dunbar's Gallery.* $50-100 for pair.

They're dull, but they can be put up in anyone's basement or garage.

Pair of Texaco Men's & Ladies' rest room keyhole shaped enamel on steel key tags, Texaco logo, with chains, 3-1/2" x 6". *Courtesy of Dunbar's Gallery.* $100-250.

Texaco was the first to promote "registered" restrooms across the United States, coinciding with the development of their new style white box buildings. The company had a fleet of White Patrol Chevrolets to inspect dealer restrooms. Phillips 66 also manned a unit of military style clad nurses, the Highway Hostesses, who kept tabs on its "certified" restrooms. For some reason, this whole cleanliness movement sort of petered out, probably because there were more important restrooms to inspect during World War II.

WOMEN'S ROOM

Union 76 Women's Room porcelain sign, 12" x 13". *Courtesy of Dunbar's Gallery.* $100-350.

A very nice sign. The only giveaway that it's Union 76 is the "property of" stamp in the lower right corner.

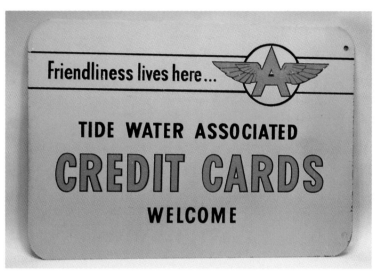

Sanitary Rest Rooms porcelain sign, 30" x 15". *Courtesy of Dunbar's Gallery.* $50-200.

Tide Water Associated Flying A Credit Cards steel sign, 1950s, double sided, 20" x 14". *Courtesy of Dunbar's Gallery.* $100-350.
Isn't it amazing what life a little logo gives to a sign?

Shell Charge Cards Honored porcelain sign, double sided, circa 1930s, 14" x 19". *Courtesy of Dunbar's Gallery.* Scarce, $200-600.
This is another category that was not collected until recently. Now collectors seek out interesting examples of credit card signs, which first were implemented in the 1930s, but really came into vogue in the 1950s. This sign is difficult to find.

GMAC National Credit Service porcelain sign, 1930s, double sided, 24" x 12". *Courtesy of Dunbar's Gallery.* $100-450.
It's scary to think about the impact of the automobile on industry. So many businesses have some automotive tie-in. One theory about the Depression is that car companies made too many cars in the 1920s and sold too many on time. There was a glut so companies had to cut back, which hurt related industries, which made stocks plummet, ...

143

Bibliography

Anderson, Scott. *Check the Oil*. Radnor, Pennsylvania: Wallace-Homestead Book Co., 1986.

Appleyard, John. *The Farm Tractor*. North Pomfret, Vermont: David & Charles, 1987.

Aune, Al. *Arcade Toys*. Brooklyn Park, Minnesota: Robert F. Mannella, 1990.

Barrett, Noel. *Automobilia and Petroliana at Auction: The Bob & Judy Palmerino Collection*. Noel Barrett Auctions, April 12, 1997.

Benjamin, Scott, and Wayne Henderson. *Oil Company Signs: A Collector's Guide*. Osceola, Wisconsin: Motorbooks International, 1995.

Bishop, George. *Classic Cars*. New York: Crescent Books, 1979.

Boylan, James. *The World and the '20s*. Dial Press, 1973.

Boyne, Walter J. *Power Behind the Wheel: Creativity and the Evolution of the Automobile*. New York: Stewart, Tabori & Chang, 1988.

Coffey, Frank, and Joseph Layden. *America on Wheels: The First 100 Years, 1896-1996*. Los Angeles: General Publishing Group, 1996.

Dalrymple, Helen, and Charles Goodrum. *Advertising: The First 200 Years*. New York: Harry N. Abrams, Inc., 1990.

Encyclopedia of American Automobiles. Edited by G. N. Georgano. New York: EP Dutton & Co., 1968.

The Encyclopedia of Collectibles. Edited by Andrea DiNoto. Chicago: Time-Life Books, 1980.

Gottschalk, Lillian. *American Toy Cars & Trucks*. New York: Abbeville Press, 1985.

Hake, Ted, and Russ King. *Price Guide to Collectible Pinback Buttons, 1886-1986*. Radnor, Pennsylvania: Wallace-Homestead Book Co., 1986.

Hambleton, Ronald. *The Branding of America*. Camden, Maine: Yankee Books, 1987.

Jacobs, Charles M. *Kenton Toys*. Atglen, Pennsylvania: Schiffer Publishing, 1996.

Langworth, Richard M. *Encyclopedia of American Cars 1930-1980*. New York: Beekman House, 1984.

Nash, Jay Robert. *Almanac of World Crime*. New York: Anchor Press/Doubleday, 1981.

The New Grolier Multimedia Encyclopedia. Online Computer Systems, 1993.

The 30's: A Time To Remember. Edited by Don Congdon. New York: Simon & Schuster, 1962.

Wallis, Michael. *Route 66: The Mother Road*. New York: St. Martin's Press, 1990.

Wallechinsky, David. *The People's Almanac Presents the 20th Centur: The Definite Compendium*. Aurum Press, 1996

Witzel, Michael Karl. *The American Gas Station*. Osceola, Wisconsin: Motorbooks International, 1992

The Guiness Book of World Records, 1998. Guinness Publishing, Ltd., 1998

Resources

Autopia Auctions
Win Maynard
15209 N.E. 90th Street
Redmond, WA 98052
Phone - 425-883-SOLD
Fax - 425-867-5568

Noel Barrett Antiques & Auctions
PO Box 300
Carversville, PA 18913
Phone 215-297-5109
Fax 215-297-0457

Dunbar's Junkyard Gallery
Howard, Martha, and Leila Dunbar
76 Haven Street
Milford, Mass. 01757
Phone 508-634-8697
Fax 508-634-8698
Email address - Dunbar2bid@aol.com